# CAREERS IN
# PRO SPORTS

By
*CORDNER NELSON*

*The Rosen Publishing Group, Inc.*
NEW YORK

Published in 1990, 1992, 1996, 1999 by The Rosen Publishing Group, Inc.
29 East 21st Street, New York, NY 10010

*Cover photo © Reutgers/Latif/Archive Photos.*

**Library of Congress Cataloging-in-Publication Data**

Nelson, Cordner.
  Careers in pro sports/by Cordner Nelson.
  Includes bibliographical references and index.
  Summary: Looks at careers in professional sports—the possibilities, life, training, and salaries, as well as career alternatives to actually playing.
   ISBN 0-8239-2896-9
   1. Sports - Vocational guidance - United States - Juvenile literature. [1. Sports - Vocational guidance. 2. Vocational guidance.] I. Title.
   GV583.N36 1996                                    89-37641
                                                      CIP
                                                      AC

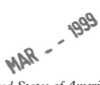

*Manufactured in the United States of America*

# About the Author

Cordner Nelson studied to be a coach, but World War II disrupted his plans. Instead, he became founding editor of *Track & Field News* in 1948 and subsequently was elected to the Track and Field Hall of Fame as a journalist rather than as an athlete or coach.

Nelson is the author of a sports novel, *The Miler,* and one of the few bestsellers about track, *The Jim Ryun Story.* He has also written two other biographical books, *Track & Field: The Great Ones* and *Track's Greatest Champions.* His 1973 history, *Runners and Races: 1,500/Mile,* was updated twelve years later to *The Milers.* He is the author of two books on training, *The Advanced Running Book* for middle- and long-distance runners and *Excelling in Sports/How to Train* for all sports. Most recently he has written articles on track and field for two encyclopedias, *World Book* and *Americana.*

Nelson says, "I know what I'm writing about from sad experience when I advise young athletes to follow their natural abilities rather than their emotions. My emotions directed me to be a distance runner, but my ability won few races. I should have put all that effort into golf or tennis or some other accuracy sport. I think this is the most important advice in this book: Don't be as dumb as I was."

# Contents

# 1

# The Exciting World of Sports

Sports play a very important role in many people's lives. Your memories of your childhood may involve a sport. You may remember throwing a baseball back and forth with your father or your best friend. Or you may remember running around your block with your friends to see who runs the fastest. Some of you may even have dreams of making a career out of your favorite sport. You dream of becoming the best in your sport, getting million-dollar contracts, and having millions of fans around the world.

For some people, this dream may come true. Perhaps you will be the next Michael Jordan or Wayne Gretzky. To succeed as a professional athlete, hard work, dedication, and talent are only some of the qualities a person needs. In this book we will discuss many of today's popular sports, their key players, and what it takes to succeed in professional sports. The world of professional sports is very competitive. There are many out there with the same dream as you. But before we can further discuss the world of professional sports, it's important to discuss why sports are so important in many people's lives.

## SPORTS AND CHILDREN
Sports become a part of many of our lives at an early age. Children naturally have a lot of energy. They run, jump,

1

and throw when playing and having fun. Although they may not realize it, this is one of the first steps children take in preparing their bodies for sports. The physical activity keeps their bodies in shape and helps muscles to grow and develop while improving coordination and agility.

They then learn about sports. They begin to participate in sports in school, or they watch it on television. They begin to form opinions about sports—what they do like and what they don't like. Many children often discover that participating in a certain sport gives them a chance to hang out with their friends or meet new friends. Participating in sports also gives children a sense of accomplishment.

They begin competing with friends to test who is faster or stronger or who can do something better. This is also another aspect of sports: to be the best or to win. However, some people believe that competition is unhealthy, especially in young children. They believe that competition puts too much pressure on children to win. But competition is a part of life. People naturally try to improve themselves to get ahead in life. Sports teach children that fair competition can bring out the best in them. Sports also teach children to accept loss as a part of life. Children soon realize that trying their best gives them a greater sense of accomplishment than winning does. In addition, many sports involve teams. Being part of a team and working together to achieve a goal teaches children cooperation and interdependence.

A child's love for a sport outweighs the possibility of loss. A child would rather play and lose than not play at all. Sometimes the goal of some athletes is just to participate or finish rather than win. For example, some athletes may be thrilled just to qualify to compete in the

Olympics. Others are triumphant when they merely finish a marathon because they are really competing against themselves.

## A PROFESSIONAL CAREER

As children become older, they may find that their changing social lives do not allow time for sports. They may find other things more important than sports. Some may begin participating in other sports to please people, such as parents. Some guys may join the school football or basketball team to impress girls. But then there are those who begin to realize how much they love their sport. They may even want to make a career out of their sport. Not everyone dreams of becoming rich and famous as a professional athlete; some just want to participate in the sport they enjoy. Whatever your goal, this book will try to help you achieve it by giving you the information you need to make the best choices for your career. It will discuss the many aspects of a career in professional sports and what you need to get started.

Before you can prepare for a career in professional sports, you need to know what you're getting into. There are good and bad aspects to every career. You need to know the pros and cons of professional sports and decide if a career in professional sports is something you want and are able to handle.

In chapter 2, the many rewards, such as fortune and fame, attached to a career in professional sports are discussed. But along with those rewards come negative aspects. The negative side of professional sports is discussed in chapter 3.

If after reading these two chapters you decide that you want a career in professional sports, you then need to prepare and plan for your future. Chapter 4 discusses various strategies and plans you can use in achieving your goal. Chapters 5 and 6 will help you to better train your body and mind to excel in your sport.

But before you can truly succeed as a professional, you will first have a long career as an amateur. As an amateur, there will be many issues that you will have to deal with, such as school, whether it be high school or college, scholarships, and even drugs. Chapter 7 will deal with many of those issues. When you are ready to turn professional, Chapter 8 will help you achieve that goal. Chapter 9 provides some helpful information about how to manage your professional career.

No matter how good you are, a professional athlete's career lasts only so long. Every professional athlete must face the day when he or she will no longer be able to compete. However, many athletes will want to stay with their sport. Every sport has many nonplaying jobs. These positions are less competitive but still offer the excitement of the sport. Chapter 10 discusses some of these jobs and how you can get them.

Chapter 11 discusses some possibilities for the future of professional sports.

No matter what kind of role you want to play in sports, amateur or professional, the field offers many valuable rewards. Participating in a sport is a fun way to keep in shape, physically and mentally, and it teaches you how to work together as a team to achieve a common goal. Sports also give you an opportunity to go out and meet new people. President Franklin D. Roosevelt once said, "Sports is the very fiber of all we stand for, it keeps our spirits alive."

# Professional Sports and Its Rewards

There is no doubt that a career in professional sports offers many rewards. You see it on television or read about it in the newspapers. Contracts are signed for millions of dollars in addition to the millions paid to athletes to endorse products. There is also the appealing aspect of being famous and having fans all over the world. As a professional athlete, you would most likely travel widely and meet many people. Then there are the physical rewards as well. Most professional sports require an athlete to stay in top physical condition. In addition, an athlete receives the best health care available. All this will help you to live a long, healthy life.

There are also many opportunities for an athlete after he or she retires. These opportunities include non-playing roles in his or her sport. For example, many athletes go on to become managers, sportscasters, or trainers after their retirement. Others go on to be spokespeople for companies, or they may write an inspiring book for their fans.

## EARNING POTENTIAL
The amount of money paid to professional athletes today is astounding. Your chances of earning a lot of

money are better in pro sports than in any other profession. The salaries paid to athletes also increase every year. One of the biggest reasons for this is the extreme popularity of sports. Fans are ready to spend their money on tickets to see their favorite athletes in competition. These fans also buy products that their favorite athlete endorses. An example of the popularity of sports can be seen in the many millions that television networks are willing to pay for the right to telecast certain sports events. The following is a list of how much the National Broadcasting Company (NBC) intends to pay for the right to broadcast the Olympic Games until the year 2008:

Winter   2000   $715 million
Summer 2002   $555 million
Winter   2006   $613 million
Summer 2008   $894 million

This is in addition to the $401 million it paid to broadcast the 1992 Games.

The reason that television networks such as NBC are willing to pay so much money for broadcasting sports events is the huge public interest. When there is a guaranteed audience watching one program, TV stations can charge companies thousands to millions of dollars to show commercials during the program. The commercials advertise products that the companies want you to buy. Everyone makes money from this, including athletes. Recent negotiations have a good percentage of this money going back to the athletes.

An increasing number of athletes are making salaries of more than $1 million. According to *Sport 100,* which lists the 100 highest-paid athletes, in 1983 only twenty-three athletes were earning more than a million dollars.

By 1987 about 118 athletes were making that much. With today's increasing salaries for professional athletes, a million dollars is nothing in 1998.

To understand the huge sums of money professional athletes are paid, it helps to know some of the annual salaries of other workers in the United States. Here are some income figures for various occupations:

| | |
|---|---|
| President of the United States | $200,000 |
| Associate Justice, Supreme Court | $164,100 |
| Member of Congress | $120,800 |
| Four-star general | $ 90,705 |
| Average income in USA | $ 31,200 |
| 52 X 40-hour week @ $5.15 | $ 10,712 |

*1997 Highest Paid Athletes*

| | |
|---|---|
| Michael Jordan | $36 million for 1 year |
| Greg Maddux | $57.5 million for 5 years |
| Steve Young | $45 million for 6 years |
| Joe Sakic | $21 million for 3 years |

The following sections look at the athletes who make the most money in their sport:

**Auto Racing:** Dale Earnhardt is the top money-maker in auto racing. His career earnings total over $28 million. Although Earnhardt won only $3.6 million, he received $15.5 million in endorsements. Between 1997 and 1998, Jeff Gordon won three of the four NASCAR Winston Cup majors. His winnings in these three races earned him over $1 million, but he also received a $1 million bonus for winning three of the four races.

7

**Baseball:** Despite talk of trying to curb baseball's rising salaries, some of the most outrageous deals were made in 1997. Outfielder Albert Belle signed a contract with the Chicago White Sox for an astounding $55 million for five years. Belle's salary topped baseball's highest salary by $2.5 million and made him the highest-paid baseball player in history. But before the season was over, two more deals surpassed Belle's. In February, the Giants signed Barry Bonds to a $11.45 million a year contract. In August, Atlanta's pitcher Greg Maddux signed a five-year deal worth $57.5 million. His annual salary of $11.5 million nearly doubled his old salary of $5.8 million. Not since Roger Clemens in 1991 had a pitcher received baseball's biggest contract.

**Basketball:** With about 400 players in the National Basketball Association (NBA), professional basketball is the most exclusive of all sports. No matter how big the baseball contracts become, they cannot surpass the deals made in basketball. Huge TV contracts allow the league to pay its players higher salaries. The league also requires a minimum pay of approximately $242,000 for rookies and $272,500 for non-rookies. Michael Jordan earned almost $32 million in 1997. In 1996, more than twenty-seven players earned more than $4 million. In addition to their salaries, many NBA stars also have lucrative endorsement deals.

The following is a list of players who exceed the NBA's $100 million package:

Kevin Garnett          $121 million for six years
  (Minnesota Timberwolves)
Shaquille O'Neal       $120 million for seven years
  (Los Angeles Lakers)

Alonzo Mourning     $112 million for seven years
(Miami Heat)
Shawn Kemp     $107 million for seven years
(Cleveland Cavaliers)
Juwan Howard     $100.8 million for seven years
(Washington Wizards)

On the women's side, the new WNBA pays its female athletes substantially lower salaries. Rebecca Lobo, Lisa Leslie, and Sheryl Swoops, the top players of the WNBA, were each paid $250,000.

**Bowling:** Walter Ray Williams Jr. became the first man in the Professional Bowlers Association to earn more than $2 million. Pete Weber followed in a close second with $1,987,214.

**Boxing:** Although Mike Tyson is still the career leading moneymaker in boxing, his unprofessional behavior in biting the ear of his opponent, Evander Holyfield, during a match has seriously hurt his chances of ever again making big money in boxing. In addition to being fined $3 million (10 percent of his $30 million purse), Tyson also had his license revoked for a year. Evander Holyfield earned $35 million from the fight. He earned almost $55 million in 1997. Boxing's "golden boy," Oscar De La Hoya, made $38 million in 1997.

**Football:** Despite having a league salary cap that limits team spending, National Football League (NFL) salaries continue to rise. The most lucrative, although unguaranteed, deals signed in the history of the game belonged to Steve Young, $45 million for six years; Brett Favre, $47.25 million for seven years; and Barry Sanders, $34.5 million for six years.

**Golf:** 1997 was a good year for Tiger Woods. Not only did he become the youngest nonwhite person ever to win the Masters, he also became 1997's biggest moneymaker in golf with earnings of close to $2 million. In addition, Woods also signed multimillion-dollar endorsement deals with American Express, Nike, and other companies.

**Harness Racing:** In 1996 Michael Lachance won almost $8.5 million. John Campbell has won almost $90 million to become one of the top moneymakers in his sport.

**Hockey:** Former New York Rangers captain Mark Messier joined the Vancouver Canucks for a three-year contract worth $20 million. The Colorado Avalanche were able to hold onto Joe Sakic with a three-year, $21 million deal, including a $15 million signing bonus. The New York Rangers also held onto Wayne Gretzky with a one-year contract worth $7 million.

**Horse Racing:** Jockey Jerry Baily earned more than $14 million in 1997 alone. Gary Stevens came in second with earnings of more than $12 million. Many trainers also have salaries in the millions. Trainer Richard Mandella earned more than $8 million in 1997.

**Rodeo:** Prize money has increased in this sport, although it is still far below that of many other professional sports. In the 1980s, the total prize money was only around $13 million, but today it has almost doubled to $23 million. T. J. Walter, all-time all-around champion, won $250,000 last year.

**Tennis:** Martina Hingis, the youngest person to win a Grand Slam title in this century, also became the first female athlete of any sport to earn over $3 million in one year. Pete Sampras leads the men with earnings over $6 million. In 1996, Boris Becker won the $6 million Grand Slam Cup, the richest prize in tennis.

**Track:** Still in the process of transition between amateurism and professionalism, track has few official winnings. Most track runners make their money from endorsement deals. In 1997, however, track's international governing body, the IAAF, announced that for the first time it will award prize money to the top finishers of the World Track and Field Championships. First-place winners will receive $60,000, second-place winners will receive $30,000, and third-place winners will receive $20,000. The federation said it expects to hand out approximately $19 million at seven major championships over the next two years.

## COACHES

In recent years, coaches have started earning salaries that equal those of players. Larry Bird, Basketball Hall of Fame player and former Boston Celtic player, agreed to coach the Indiana Pacers for $4.5 million a year.

Coach Rick Pitino left the University of Kentucky to coach the Boston Celtics for an astounding ten-year deal worth $70 million.

Phil Jackson, coach of the Chicago Bills, stayed another year for a $5.7 million contract.

## ENDORSEMENTS

Another way that athletes earn money in addition to salaries is through product endorsement. Many companies are willing to pay top athletes millions of dollars to endorse their products, from sneakers to soft drinks to hot dogs, because they know that consumers will buy the products endorsed by their favorite athletes.

Michael Jordan is a good example of how a star can make millions from product endorsement. In 1992, when Jordan retired from basketball, he still made $35.9 million from endorsements alone. When he returned to basketball, his income from endorsements reached $40 million. In 1997 Jordan received an estimated $47 million in endorsements. In addition, he signed a deal to produce sports apparel for Nike.

The following are some of the endorsement deals made by professional athletes:

- Grant Hill of the Detroit Pistons signed a seven-year, $80 million endorsement deal with Fila.
- Tiger Woods' endorsement deals with American Express, Nike, and other companies pay him an estimated $60 million.
- Tracy McGrady, an 18-year-old high school graduate, signed a six-year, $12 million endorsement deal with Adidas, and he hadn't even been drafted yet.

According to *Forbes* magazine, the following athletes earned the most from endorsement deals:

| | |
|---|---|
| Michael Jordan (basketball) | $47 million |
| Tiger Woods (golf) | $24 million |
| Arnold Palmer (golf) | $16 million |
| Dale Earnhardt (auto racing) | $15 million |
| Andre Agassi (tennis) | $14 million |
| Greg Norman (golf) | $13 million |
| Shaquille O'Neal (basketball) | $12.5 million |
| Grant Hill (basketball) | $12 million |

In addition to salaries and endorsement deals, some athletes also open their own businesses. A group of athletes, including Andre Agassi and Ken Griffey Jr., combined their efforts and opened a chain of restaurants called The All-Star Café. Shaquille O'Neal recently opened his own restaurant. In addition, O'Neal has also released a rap album and starred in two motion pictures. Michael Jordan also starred in the blockbuster motion picture *Space Jam*.

As a professional athlete, you will have more free time than in most other jobs. Your working days are shorter, and you have an off-season of three to six months. Several pros have gone through medical school in their spare time while earning large salaries. Chi Chi Rodriguez said of Jack Nicklaus, "He's the only golfer in history who became a living legend in his spare time."

Professional athletes have many possible careers after their retirement from the sport. They've earned enough money to retire or study for a different career. The fame they had during their pro career will always be with them, giving them opportunities and opening doors in whatever they choose to do.

You will benefit from better health. Athletes have to be in peak physical condition, so part of your effort will go into learning to protect and improve your body. Long ago, Benjamin Franklin said, "Games lubricate the body and the mind," and today the benefits of exercise are widely known.

For anybody who loves to play and is good enough for the pros, it would be difficult to find a better job.

# The Dark Side of Pro Sports

You may be thinking, what's the catch? It's true that pro sports can offer you a glamorous life full of wealth, fame, and fun. But you have heard only one side of the story. A career in pro sports can also bring you disillusionment, heartbreak, and failure. Before you go much further, you should take a realistic look at the dark side of pro sports.

## Catch #1: Tough Competition

The very same rewards that make a sports career so desirable also put it out of reach of most athletes. Millions of young athletes dream of the glamorous life, but there is room for only a few to succeed. Consider some statistics:

Only about 1,500 positions are open in the National Football League. Basketball is even more limited, with only about 350 NBA jobs. There are only 700 Major League Baseball players. Golf has a little more than 200 on tour. Of the million high school football players, only about 150 make it to the NFL. Of the half million basketball players in high school, about fifty will make an NBA team. Mathematically, the odds are 6,000 to one against making the NFL and 10,000 to one for the NBA.

Former pro footballer Norm Van Brocklin said, "There's no tougher way to make easy money than pro football."

## CATCH #2: INJURIES

In some sports, notably football, the possibility of injury is a constant threat. Before each week's games the NFL releases a list of dozens of players who are injured. Some of them play despite their injuries. A few are out for the whole season. An outstanding player might be kept under contract while missing a whole season, but more often his career ends without a chance to show his true worth.

No figures are available as to how many players are lost because of injuries. Beginning in high school, many players drop out because of injuries, and even more drop out of college sports. Of the 5.8 million high school athletes, an estimated 1 million are injured each year. It is no fun to play a game if you are injured time after time. What's worse, your chances of gaining a college scholarship or a pro contract are much less if you are injury-prone.

Sports medicine authorities say that a certain amount of brain injury is inevitable in boxing, football, and soccer.

Roger Craig, the great running back for the San Francisco 49ers, suffered much wear and tear in a game. He said, "After a game I look like I've been locked in a cage with a tiger." He has imprints of face masks on his back, gouges from turf burns on his arms, and bruises from cleats on his hands. "I can sense there's internal bleeding from all the blows and bruises because for several hours my body temperature is very warm. I can't eat that night, and I have difficulty sleeping."

Richard Todd, quarterback for the New York Jets, tells about a 1981 game: "I don't know if I should tell you this, but I was injected [with pain killers] six times in my front and five times in my back just prior to that game. Then at halftime I got shot up in the ribs and the cartilage again."

Dr. James Parker, team physician for the New York Mets, says, "Every time a man pitches, he is systematically injuring his arm. A pitcher's durability will depend on the genetic capacity of the arm to recover from the insult of pitching."

In the 1970s, the Canadian Ophthalmological Society found thirty-seven Canadian pro hockey players who were blind in one eye from playing injuries.

If you have more than your share of injuries, give serious consideration to specializing in a different sport.

## CATCH #3: LACK OF FREEDOM

Even if you break into a pro sport, your contract binds you to one team for a number of years. If you do not like the coach or he does not like you, chances are that you will sit on the bench more than you like. If you do not like the city that is your new home, you cannot change it. You may have to put up with a situation you dislike for five years before you have any freedom of choice.

Your team can cut you or trade you to another team, and you have no rights at all. You often have no choice but to do as you are told until you have been there enough years to become a free agent. You may have to play while injured, risking your future career.

If you are a superstar and get along with everybody, none of this will happen, but a large number of professional athletes suffer from a lack of freedom.

Famous professional athletes are much like celebrities such as movie stars in that once they become a household name, they no longer have the freedom to come and go as they please. Many professional athletes cannot even leave their houses without being mobbed by fans who want autographs or pictures. In a sense, their life no longer belongs to them; it belongs to the public. That's the price of fame and fortune.

## CATCH #4: LIFE ON THE ROAD

People who have never been away from home tend to glamorize travel more than people who travel do. After a game, sometimes near midnight, players have to ride a bus to an airport, wait for their plane, fly for up to five hours, and then ride another bus to a hotel. It is not a restful night.

Major-league baseball players do this about thirty times each season. Basketball players travel even more, but football players travel to only eight away games plus a few exhibition games. Golfers travel as much as baseball players, and tennis players travel most of all.

If you do not like to fly, or if you cannot sleep on a plane, these trips can feel like a real hardship. Add the lack of regular hours for sleeping, a poor choice of food, and few hours of free time and you have a life you might not choose.

## CATCH #5: WRONG LIFESTYLE

It is natural for creatures, human or animal, to adapt themselves to their environment. The environment of young, energetic athletes, given sudden wealth and separated from the good influences of their hometown and family, tends to lead many of them astray.

Peter Gent, a former football pro who wrote *North Dallas Forty,* said, "Athletes hang around with people who tell them, 'The rules don't apply to you.'" Don Reese confessed in a *Sports Illustrated* article in 1982: "Cocaine arrived in my life with my first-round draft into the NFL in 1974. It has dominated my life. Eventually, it took control and almost killed me. Cocaine may be found in quantity throughout the NFL. It's pushed on players. Sometimes it's pushed by players. Just as it controlled me, it now controls and corrupts the game, because so many players are on it."

Another loss is often the joy of a young family. Professional athletes are away from home almost as much as sailors. If you are married, it becomes a hardship for both you and your spouse. If you have children, it is hard on them and lonely for you.

## CATCH #6: LOSS OF DESIRE TO PLAY

For one reason or another, your sport can become tiresome instead of fun.

A game you play for fun can become a job where you are continually looking over your shoulder at somebody who wants to take it away from you. In college if you go into a slump for a while, the worst that can happen to you is some bench time. As a pro you might lose your job and not find another. For some athletes that means constant fear, and that can take the joy out of playing. Or you might simply outgrow your sport. Your values change as you grow older, and you might find some activity you would rather do. Or, as with many other activities, too much of a good thing may simply wear out your enjoyment of it.

Roger Maris of the Yankees hit sixty-one homers in 1961, and it left him a bitter man: "They did everything they could to downgrade them. They acted as though I was doing something wrong, poisoning the record books or something. Do you know what I have to show for the sixty-one home runs? Nothing. Exactly nothing."

Bernie Parent, former goalie for the Philadelphia Flyers, said, "There is a built-in discipline to playing any sport, a structure that keeps you within certain bounds. I played hockey for twenty-five years. All of a sudden, I couldn't play anymore. The discipline was gone."

If your game is no longer fun, you'll do it solely for the rewards—money and fame. The catch is, you won't do it as well and you will lose the rewards sooner.

## CATCH #7: SHORT PLAYING CAREER

You have heard of durable athletes competing until the age of forty. If you continue to earn a large salary, and if you invest properly, you will not need to work for money for the rest of your life. But what are your chances of playing until you are forty? If you play at all—sign a contract—you will have, on the average, a career of less than five years! The average player in baseball, football, basketball, and hockey lasts less than five years.

A short career in itself is no reason to decide against trying, but the strong possibility of short-lived success means you should think hard about what else you will do with your life. For many pros, life after sports is a hard letdown. Fame evaporates rapidly, and suddenly you must adjust your self-esteem and take your place among the common people.

## CATCH #8: UNCERTAIN INCOME

Once you have signed a contract, you know how much you will be paid for the duration of that contract. You do not know if you will ever receive another contract. And some contracts provide for termination if you do not perform at an expected level.

In many sports your income is in the form of prize money. Golfers, tennis players, bowlers, and rodeo riders all must perform well to have any income at all. They must win enough money to pay for their food and lodging and their travel expenses to the next tournament. It is said that a pro golfer must win at least $25,000 each year to pay for the minimum of expenses.

## CATCH #9: UNDERDEVELOPMENT

The harder you work at becoming a great athlete, and the more time and thought you devote to it, the less time and thought you will give to other activities. Other ambitions you may have will be delayed or canceled. It is possible to delay an important career until after your pro sports career, but it is much more difficult. Senator Bill Bradley did it, waiting to enter politics until after his basketball career ended. Many athletes are too content with their income and lifestyle, and they often have nothing to fall back on when their career is over.

## CATCH #10: STRESS

Psychiatrist Grigori Raiport says, "The professional athlete has more stress than the average person. Every third athlete suffers an adverse effect from stress. They are more stress-resistant than the average person, but still every third of them breaks down."

These are definite disadvantages, but for most athletes they do not outweigh the strong attraction of a pro career. If you have the athletic ability and the necessary mental toughness and if you love your sport, then go for it. This is not a situation where you risk everything and surrender all other opportunities in life. Fortunately, a career in pro sports begins with amateur sports. You can enjoy sports through high school and college while you prepare for another career just as if you had never heard of professional sports. Then, if you are good enough and if you want to, you can decide to try for a professional career. You can have the best of both worlds!

# Choose Your Strategy

If you decide to try for a career in professional sports, you want to know how to go about it. You need some sort of plan to keep you headed in the right direction. A little advance planning will save you a lot of wrong turns and headaches.

Before you make an outline of a tentative plan, you need to do a little thinking about what is involved. Think about these questions:

## HOW DO YOU BECOME A GREAT ATHLETE?

Are great athletes born or made? The answer is—both. You need both great natural ability and the ideal environment to become a great athlete. Think about it this way: You were born with a certain amount of potential ability. Nothing you ever do will make you better than that potential. Everything you do after being born determines how close you come to reaching your potential.

To visualize this situation, start at the bottom of a piece of paper and draw a rectangle one inch wide. The height of the rectangle determines the total area. That is your potential. If your rectangle is only six inches high and somebody else has a rectangle ten inches high, you will be at a disadvantage. Now fill in your rectangle, starting from the bottom, to represent how much you have progressed toward your potential. If you accomplish the maximum progress, your rectangle will be full. If the other athlete's rectangle is only half full, it will reach only five inches high while yours is six, and you will win, even though you started out with less potential.

You cannot do anything to improve the height of your rectangle, but you can take two equally important steps: (1) You can choose the sport in which your rectangle is high enough to give you a chance, and (2) you can develop yourself so that your rectangle is almost full. If you find a sport in which your natural potential is adequate and if you work to reach that potential, you will become a good athlete.

One of the great secrets of sports is the fact that although you cannot increase the potential you were born with, you can maximize it. Each sport requires different abilities. The secret is to choose the sport in which you have the greatest ability and to refine your skills with constant practice.

## How Do You Exploit Your Natural Ability?

You were born with certain natural attributes. Some of those must be much better than average if you hope to be a professional athlete. Luckily, one strong quality, intensely developed, is enough to turn you into a pro. Your main problem—the single most important decision you'll ever make with regard to playing a professional sport—is to select your best sport.

It is undoubtedly true that thousands of potentially great athletes never play seriously at their best sport. There are probably hundreds of basketball players not quite good enough for the NBA who could have ranked near the top in tennis. There are many marginal football players who could have been great in track and field. For every good professional player, there is probably someone with similar natural ability who never tried that sport.

Why? There are many reasons: (1) People aim for the high-paying sports where the competition is much tougher. (2) People fall in love with a sport and devote all their time to it instead of to a sport in which they have more ability. (3) Some lack opportunity, such as inner-city kids who spend hours shooting baskets and never see a golf course nor belong to a tennis club. (4) Parents often direct their children to other goals, many of them outside of sports. (5) Many never develop their ability because they don't know it is there, or they have not learned to like that sport.

One of the saddest stories in sports is the player who works hard under the wise direction of a good coach and yet never approaches greatness because he or she is in the wrong sport. Your most important obligation to yourself is to aim in the right direction.

Pepper Martin of the St. Louis Cardinals once said, "You can take an ol' mule and run him and feed him and train him and get him in the best shape of his life, but you ain't going to win the Kentucky Derby."

The most common way to find your best sport is to try many sports to learn where your talents fit best. The main drawback is that it takes a year or two of playing and practicing to learn some of the skills, and so you have time for no more than a few sports. A better way is to think about your natural attributes and choose a few sports accordingly. Consider these:

- Your height. Surprisingly, few sports require greater than average height, although it is an advantage in some. If you are on the short side you should not fall in love with basketball unless you are one in a million as a long shooter and extremely fast and agile.

- Your weight. Even more surprisingly, your weight is less decisive than your height because you have more control over it. Football linemen must be large, but your natural weight plus a little added weight from strength training will do for almost all other sports.
- Your strength. Few sports require great natural strength. You can develop enough strength for all the others. Natural strength is necessary for a fastball pitcher, for football linemen, and for wrestling and boxing.
- Your speed. Running speed is about 90 percent natural. If you are slow of foot, you cannot play half of the football positions, and you will not reach the top in baseball, basketball, track, or soccer.
- Your quickness. This may be the single most important ability in sports. Apart from running speed, quickness means how fast you can react and begin the correct movement. You must be quick to change directions in reaction to your opponent. You must have fast muscles to put speed into such diverse movements as a tennis serve, a golf swing, and a left hook. Only a few sports do not need quickness, notably billiards, bowling, marathon running, and the all-important short game in golf.
- Your agility. Quickness means that you can start fast and move fast once you start. Agility means

that you can make the movements correctly. The two should go together. If you are especially agile, you can be a baseball shortstop, a basketball playmaker, a boxer, a wrestler, or a racquetball player. You can judge your agility in such sports by how fast you can learn such skills as juggling, typing, dancing, skating, or playing Ping Pong.

- Your accuracy. You need special natural ability—in addition to much practice—to be a good passer, pitcher, putter, shooter, or placekicker. You need it in the offensive part of soccer and hockey. You can test your accuracy easily by comparing yourself to others in your ability to hit targets with any kind of ball or with darts or even rocks.

- Your endurance. You can develop much endurance, but you need the basis of exceptional natural endurance to be good as a marathon runner, cyclist, boxer, or soccer player. It will make you better at basketball, hockey, football, and tennis. You can judge your natural endurance only by comparing yourself with others who have had the same amount of training. If you tire more quickly than average, avoid the endurance sports.

- Your cooperation. In team sports you must cooperate, sometimes at a sacrifice to your personal record. For example, in basketball, do you try to add to your point total by shooting an eighteen-footer, or do you pass to a teammate with an easier shot? Rick Barry, who once made nineteen assists in one game as a forward, said, "A lot of

players don't know what it is to make a pass. It's not that they don't know how; it's just that they're not looking for anybody." If you have trouble cooperating, try an individual sport.
- Your desire. The "hungry" athlete wins—if all else is close to equal. Your enthusiasm for what you are doing, in sports or anything else, determines how hard you are willing to work, how much time you will work, and how efficiently you will work. If you have a passion for one activity you will probably work extra hours at it, and so you will not have those extra hours for anything else. Unfortunately, time is limited.

Unless you have extraordinary natural ability, you will not be a great success in sports, or most activities, without this passion that drives you to work hard. Therefore, if your talents lie in one direction and your interests in another, you have a problem. You must choose between what you want and what you can have. Fortunately, you are likely to find the two are identical much of the time, but avoid the mistake of trying to be a square peg in a round hole.

## YOUR DECISION

You don't have to decide right away. The younger you are, the longer you can wait. But you should begin the process of narrowing down your choices. With the help of your parents, teachers, coaches, and friends you can begin to find your strengths and weaknesses. By the time you start high school you should narrow your sports down to about five, such as three team sports and two individual. That is not an inflexible rule, but you will find it difficult to keep up with more. It does not mean that you cannot change during high school. You might try another sport for fun and like it enough to add it. Or you might suddenly have the opportunity to try a new sport, such as if your parents join a tennis club. But you will probably have to drop another sport to make room for the new one.

By the time you reach your senior year of high school, you should be thinking of college scholarships, and so you will select one or two sports. The others will be eliminated, perhaps forever, or relegated to a weekend or summer recreation.

For most of your school career—high school and college—you can compete in one or more sports just like any other school athlete. Near your senior year in college you can decide about trying for a professional career. If you do not, you will have had your fun and competition, with perhaps a scholarship and all the other benefits. Thus, you have everything to gain and almost nothing to lose. Go for it!

## MAXIMIZE YOUR POTENTIAL

Once you have found your best sport, you can reach your maximum of potential ability by using many parts of your environment. Your parents can help by providing you with opportunity, such as joining a golf club or driving you to the skating rink. Family support is almost a necessity for success in sports. Your coaches can aid you immeasurably by teaching you skills, by directing your conditioning, by giving you good advice, and by providing inspirational leadership. You can also be helped by other people, by good health habits, and by books and films. But by far the most important aid to your attempt to fulfill your maximum potential can be summed up in a single word—effort.

## TRY

Many potentially great athletes have the other environmental advantages, but many of them fall short because they do not try as hard as they can. Perhaps they were superstars in high school and college, and they continue to believe that their 80 percent effort is all it takes. Some athletes have so much natural ability that they stop trying before they reach their potential. This phenomenon is seen most easily in track. A world record is thought of as the ultimate, and most athletes who break a world record think they have gone about as far as they can go. But if you think back to when Roger Bannister first ran a mile under four minutes or Parry O'Brien first put the shot over sixty feet, you will see that nobody thought more effort would lead to many miles under 3:50 and many shot puts over seventy feet.

Other successful athletes are lazy, content to be good without going all out to be their best. Many do not know all the different ways they can try in order to improve. Most try hard in some ways but neglect others. To be truly great, an athlete must try as hard as possible in every way he knows and then try to find other ways. Joe DiMaggio said, "No boy from a rich family ever made the big leagues."

You don't have to look far to find examples of success as a result of trying. Do you remember when you learned to ride a bicycle? You simply kept trying until, as if by magic, you learned to balance. Do you know how jugglers learn to keep seven objects in the air with their two hands? They do it by trying for thousands of hours. A concert pianist plays the piano several hours a day for many years. You may envy a pro basketball player who earns a few hundred thousand a year for his shooting ability. Do you have any idea how many thousands of shots he practiced?

Jim Ryun became an "overnight" sensation as a sixteen-year-old sophomore. Few people knew that he had run an average of twelve miles a day for the previous year through rain, snow, and Kansas heat until often he could not eat his dinner. He tried as few athletes have ever tried, before or since.

Johnny Bench won Rookie of the Year honors, and people thought he was just naturally great. They didn't know that his father was a catcher, that Johnny decided he wanted to be a ball player when he was seven, and that his father drilled him by the hour in throwing from the crouch to each base and fielding bunts and pop fouls.

Wayne Gretzky, possibly the greatest of all hockey players, had a father who taught him to skate when he was two. He practiced hockey for hours, and at five he played against ten-year-olds. He became a pro at seventeen and has been named hockey's Most Valuable Player nine times.

Tiger Woods' interest in golf started when he was only six months old. By the time he was six, he was featured in *Golf Digest*. Nancy Lopez won a golf tournament at nine. The list goes on and on. Trying makes it happen.

Steve Garvey, the National League's Most Valuable Player in 1974, said, "The harder we work, the more it becomes a habit, and we learn that hard work turns into success."

## IF YOU DON'T PLAY, WHAT ELSE CAN YOU DO?

If you love sports but lack the natural ability to be a professional athlete, or if you don't want to try, you can go into one of the many nonplaying jobs in sports.

Most of the fame and fortune from pro sports go to the athletes, but there are more jobs related to sports for nonplayers. Many athletes, whether or not they are good enough for the glamour jobs, go on to lifetime jobs in the sports they love. Here are some sports-related jobs you might consider.

**Coaching.** Every team, from high school to the pros, has one or more coaches. In any given year in the United States, no more than about 5,000 professional athletes make a living as players, but there are more than 160,000 coaches. A coach must be an expert at the sport and a good leader.

**Trainers.** Although fewer in number than coaches, trainers have more secure jobs with far less stress. Trainers must learn as much as a doctor does about sports injuries.

**Sportswriters.** Each newspaper usually has one to several full- or part-time sportswriters, and there are about 10,000 newspapers. Sportswriters usually know and love several sports.

**Administrators.** Sports need people to smooth the path, all the way from the commissioners of football and baseball down to the people who distribute tickets. Athletic directors are the best-known administrators, but there are many others.

**Announcers.** Radio and television announcers are a prominent part of sports because more people listen to or watch sports broadcasts than go to the stadium. Only a few jobs are available in this field.

## MAKE YOUR PLAN

At this point you can begin making a general plan for your sports career. You can use a notebook, adding and changing goals as you go along. You can use the same notebook to keep a record of your progress in training and competition.

To begin with, your general plan should look something like this:

1. Decide which sports to try (chapter 4).
2. Begin playing.
3. Learn to study so you'll be eligible for school sports.
4. Learn how to train (chapter 5).
5. Learn how to compete (chapter 6).
6. Manage your amateur career (chapter 7).
7. Decide whether to try to be a pro. If not, see step number 10 on this list.
8. Work at breaking in as a pro (chapter 8).
9. Manage your professional career (chapter 9).
10. Consider a sports-related career (chapter 10).

# Train Yourself to Excel

After you have considered your natural abilities and selected a sport, you need a training plan to help you reach your potential. Training can be divided into conditioning your body and learning skills. Before you can make plans, you need to know the basics of how to condition your body and learn skills.

## CONDITIONING
Conditioning involves improving your strength, speed, quickness, and endurance.

Before you consider each of those areas of improvement, you should think about how your body changes.

Your body changes as a response to stimuli. A stimulus is anything that causes a reaction, such as the burning pain from a hot stove or a ten-mile run.

Training is the proper selection of stimuli. You stimulate your body so that it will change. There are different kinds of stimuli, but the kind you need to condition your body is stress.

Stress is caused by any stimulus that disturbs your body. When stressed, your body fights back to protect itself, and if the stress continues, your body's resistance causes permanent changes in your body. The most common example may be friction to your skin.

Your body's reaction builds a callus to protect your skin.

The art and science of training consists of selecting stresses strong enough to cause your body to improve and yet not so strong as to harm your body.

You can monitor your improvement easily. It is not so easy to be sure that you do not overtrain, even though there are many warning signs. Some of the symptoms of overtraining are fatigue, loss of enthusiasm, aches, weight loss, increased pulse rate, and decreases in your red corpuscle count and your hemoglobin values. One of the most valuable training secrets is the fact that you cannot recover fully in twenty-four hours. Most athletes now alternate hard days with easier days to avoid overtraining.

You can improve greatly if you increase stress gradually and avoid exhausting all of your adaptive energy.

The main benefits of training will be to your strength, your speed, your endurance, and your skills. Let's examine each of these, along with training efficiency.

## STRENGTH

You can be better at almost any sport by increasing your strength. Some sports, such as football, require great all-body strength. Other sports require strength in certain muscles, such as a pitcher's arm, a kicker's leg, or the muscles a batter uses to swing a bat.

A strong muscle means more speed because it can move your body faster. A strong muscle means more endurance because it needs less energy to do the same work. Almost any athlete can benefit from increased all-body strength because of increased speed and endurance.

It may help you to know a little about how muscles work. Each muscle is made up of thousands of muscle fibers in groups of 100 to 150. Each group is activated by a single motor nerve. The more power you want, the more groups are activated. For example, to hold an egg in your hand you would activate only one group. If you used all the groups you would crush the egg. When you use your muscles they become larger and stronger because each individual fiber thickens.

You can use five methods for strength training. The easiest of these is a series of exercises that use your body weight as resistance, such as push-ups and sit-ups. These are limited in the amount of strength they can build.

Isometric contractions take place when you exert your muscular power against an immovable object. Unlike exercises in which resistance is your body weight or less, isometric exercises strain your muscles to the limit. But your muscles do not move, so you can strengthen only part of each muscle.

Resistance training is designed to work your muscles using actions similar to the skill you use. Examples are the football charging sled, sprinting up a hill, and swinging a leaded bat. You can increase your strength, but you must be careful not to overdo the resistance—otherwise, you risk ruining your form.

Weight training will develop more strength and will do it faster. You should not start any heavy weight training without instruction from a competent coach because some exercises are far better for you than others, and because you need to know the correct methods and safety precautions.

Circuit training is a series of exercises made up of any of the first four types. Arrange the exercises so that you can rest one part of your body while exercising another. Circuit training can also combine flexibility exercises, which is especially valuable because you need to follow each resistance movement with a natural movement to retain your correct form.

Before starting your strength program, you should have some sort of plan. Which muscles do you want to strengthen and by how much? Most athletes begin with general strengthening and add whatever specific strength they need for their sport.

Another question to answer as part of your planning: How much body weight do you want to add? If you are a football player, a heavyweight boxer, a shot-putter, or a skinny basketball player, you probably want to add weight. If you are a marathon runner, a jockey, a soccer player, a tennis player, or a weight-class boxer, you do not want to add weight. To avoid weight gain you should use lighter weights with more repetitions and do only a minimum of general strength training.

Next you need to understand how to strengthen a muscle. Your muscle fibers grow thicker and thus stronger through a chemical reaction to the stimulus of exhaustion. Therefore, the fastest and surest way to improve your strength is to exhaust your muscles. You should select a weight you can lift about eight or ten times but not more than about fifteen times. One such set is enough each day, and you should rest for about forty-eight hours between sessions to give your fibers time to grow.

One drawback to weight training is the equipment necessary. You need access to an elaborate set of "iron" or an expensive weight machine. If you want to improvise, you can substitute wall pulleys, weighted containers, or a rope wrapped around a bar to provide controlled resistance.

If you insist on beginning without a coach, you must at least read a book. You must know the safety rules and proper technique. You also need advice on your choice of lifts. Do not use the competitive weight-lifting exercises because they are more dangerous and less valuable. You should probably start with exercises such as the clean and press, abdominal curls, the bouncing split squat, and various arm exercises with dumbbells. Then add any exercise specific to your sport. For example, a kicker wants to strengthen the muscles that flex the hip and extend the lower leg.

Circuit training is probably best for anybody, even if your only strength work is weight training. Stretch every muscle after strengthening it, and alternate the use of various parts of your body so that your legs rest while you work on your arms. And add a minute or so of "rest" while you go through the motions of your sport with no weight resistance so as to maintain your skills. Twice a week is enough weight training for maintaining strength, but you might do more for greater strength or for endurance training.

It is not at all uncommon for an athlete to increase the strength of certain muscle groups by more than 200 percent. You can improve almost any aspect of any sport through proper weight training. On the other hand, it is possible to decrease your skills through incorrect weight training, as Johnny Miller learned when his strengthened shoulder muscles ruined the rhythm of his great golf swing. Find some help and do it right.

## Speed and Quickness

Running speed is of great value in many sports. Even a football lineman has more chance at a pro contract if his speed over forty yards is faster than average. Quickness is speed of movement, not necessarily in running. A basketball player without quickness had better be close to seven feet tall, and a slow boxer had better have the strength of a grizzly bear in his arms.

Speed and quickness are natural talents. Some people are born faster than others. Most people could never learn to run fast enough to be a sprinter or a halfback, and how many people are quick enough to be a pro basketball forward or a hockey goalie? You cannot improve your speed greatly, nothing like the 300 percent possible in strength training, but you can improve 10 percent. That is one yard in ten, enough to avoid a tackle or to be safe at first base instead of out.

Even more impressive is the fact that the speed and quickness of your start and pickup can be improved the most, so that most athletes can improve 20 percent in the first few yards. Imagine how valuable it is to be two steps farther along in football, baseball, basketball, or soccer.

The best way to learn to run faster is to go out for track and learn from a professional coach. If you cannot do that and want to learn by yourself, it is not a simple process. You can run faster by increasing your leg speed, increasing the length of your stride, or both. This can be done by improving your sprinting skill and strengthening your running muscles.

The best example of the value of strength to a sprinter is Ben Johnson of Canada, who ran the two fastest 100s ever run. He spent more time than any other sprinter on weight training and enhanced it with steroids, for which he was disqualified from the 1988 Olympic Games. He looked more like a football player than a track runner, but his speed was unsurpassed.

Added strength means that you can push your body farther along with each stride, resulting in a longer stride. It means that you can push your body faster, resulting in greater leg speed. It also means that you can lift your knees faster and higher and drive your feet down at the track faster and harder. The right kind of strength adds to your speed.

A considerable amount of skill is involved in running fast. Correct running form will make you faster. The most important part of your sprinting form is the length of your stride. A shorter stride is quicker, but a longer stride covers more ground, obviously. If you lengthen your stride it takes more time. Your goal is to find the optimum length for your stride through experimentation. You can check your speed by how it feels to you, by being timed, or, best of all, by how you gain or lose alongside another sprinter maintaining a steady sprint.

Other parts of the sprinting skill include high knee action, hip flexibility, elimination of waste movement, and relaxation. If you can move your legs fast and hard while relaxing all unneeded muscles, you will not only run faster but you will save strength for your next sprint.

To be a good sprinter you also need a fast start and pickup. The shorter the race, the more important these become, so the start and pickup are vital in sports that require a short burst of speed.

Actually, a good start requires an advantageous starting position, a quick reflex, and correct form. A sprinter is allowed to use any starting position, and the sprint start has proved to be the fastest. In the sprint start, the sprinter's hands are on the track with one foot farther back than the other. After a push with both feet and a step with the back foot, the sprinter's body is leaning far forward and all the power goes forward. If you used that power while standing upright, you would fall flat on your back. Therefore, in sports where you do not have time to take the optimum starting position, you should approach it as closely as possible. A basketball or tennis player should be in a crouch rather than standing at attention. A baseball batter should learn to finish a swing with knees bent and body leaning toward first base.

A reflex action is actually more complicated than the example of jerking your hand away from a hot stove. You must learn to react to a stimulus without conscious thought. A sprinter trains with a starting pistol until his or her reaction to the sound is no longer delayed by any conscious brain activity. Nerve pathways change so that the sound of the gun seems to go directly to the legs. A basketball player must learn to react to something more complicated, such as an opponent's pass or even a movement of a foot.

The speed of your reflex is not as important as its correctness. You might have the fastest reaction on the basketball court, but if you step in the wrong direction, you are two steps behind. The most important part of starting is making the right movement. Thus, starting is a skill that requires much practice to master. Few things are as important in the quickness sports such as tennis, basketball, boxing, hockey, and soccer. When practicing, think through your movements in slow motion and work out the correct starting position and foot and arm movements. Then drill yourself on them until they become a reflex action.

Your pickup, although important, is relatively simple. The same principles apply as in sprinting full speed, except that during your pickup you adjust your body lean to your stride length. This means that you need to lean forward more when you burst into a sprint than when you are in full stride. Therefore, the skill of your pickup lies in quickly assuming the correct body lean and beginning with short steps.

In a game like soccer or basketball or tennis you spend some time standing and waiting before making a quick burst of speed. During these periods, you should be partially crouched so that your body angle will be closer to the extreme lean that you need for the fastest start and pickup. Your first movement should be with the foot farthest away from the direction you want to go, but at the same time your body should turn in that direction and lean more. If you practice those principles, your reflex action will give you a much faster start and pickup.

## ENDURANCE

There are many kinds of endurance, and the lack of any one of these kinds can cause you to lose.

In considering exactly how this applies to you, a little knowledge of physiology might help. Think of your muscle cells as little engines. They can do their work as long as they have fuel and oxygen, but instead of gasoline they need carbohydrates for fuel. Your muscles store some fuel and a tiny amount of oxygen for instant reactions, but for much of their fuel and almost all the oxygen you must rely on your blood.

The first kind of endurance to consider is aerobic. Most of your endurance falls into this category. The word aerobic means "with oxygen," so aerobic work is what you can do using the oxygen supplied by your blood. When you move fast enough to begin puffing, you are going beyond aerobic exercise into anaerobic, which means "without oxygen." Actually, you are using all the oxygen your blood can supply during anaerobic exercise, but that is not enough, so you must go into oxygen debt. Your anaerobic work is done chemically, and the amount you can go into debt is strictly limited. Even if you avoid anaerobic debt, a long session of aerobic exercise will deplete your glycogen supply, the fuel stored in your muscles. Loss of glycogen causes a marathon runner to "hit the wall" and a tennis player to lose some of his skill near the end of a long five-set match. Your muscles may also fail to get enough blood supply because you do not have enough capillaries carrying blood to them or because your hemoglobin is low and so does not carry enough oxygen. Another muscle failure results from lack of strength, because a weak muscle must work closer to its maximum capacity and so it goes into oxygen debt sooner.

If you lack aerobic endurance you will "run out of gas" in basketball, soccer, boxing, tennis, hockey, and, of course, distance running. You might even lose energy playing a mild sport like golf if you play for four or five hours.

Your aerobic endurance is really a combination of physiological functions. It is greater with a full blood supply and a full fuel supply, but the basic tool is your heart. If you do anything that increases your pulse rate for several minutes each day, your heart will adapt to the added work by growing larger and stronger. It will then be able to pump more blood with each beat, which accounts for the lower pulse rate of trained endurance athletes. Therefore, the best method of training for aerobic endurance is to be active often. The maximum gain would probably come from running for about half an hour a day at the fastest pace you can without pushing you far into oxygen debt. You would improve your aerobic endurance greatly with such a training schedule. For most sports that is enough, although a distance runner runs more in hopes of improving his or her speed.

With aerobic training, your muscles keep demanding more blood, causing you to grow more capillaries in the muscles you use regularly. A swimmer and a middle-distance runner develop similar aerobic capacities, but a swimmer tires rapidly when he tries to run because his running muscles have not developed enough capillaries to receive all the blood they need. Make certain you repeat all your movements enough to grow all the capillaries within the muscles you need. A tennis player who never serves except when playing will find it tiring to serve long games. If a boxer did not spend hours holding his arms up while punching the bag, he would be too tired to fight more than a round or two.

Another way your muscles fail to obtain enough oxygen is when your hemoglobin level drops. Hemoglobin makes up about 95 percent of the dry weight of your red blood cells and carries most of the oxygen in your blood. Red blood cells are destroyed regularly in everyday living, and hard training destroys them much faster. If you do not replace these destroyed cells, you will die. A hemoglobin value of 14 is enough for the average person, but an endurance athlete needs a value of 16 to 17 to perform well. You can build up your hemoglobin value in several ways: (1) Rest after hard training, which means at least two days of light work before a long competition. (2) Eat a balanced diet of fresh, unrefined foods that provide plenty of iron. (3) Live at high altitude. (4) Don't overtrain. You can check your blood values most accurately with a blood test, but if you feel run down you should consider the possibility.

Your anaerobic capacity allows you to go into oxygen debt, but that capacity is limited. A top-notch sprinter cannot run at full speed for more than about 300 yards. You should not try to improve your anaerobic endurance until you have enough aerobic capacity to handle the training. Sports physiologists have determined that an otherwise well-trained runner can develop his anaerobic capacity to the maximum in five weeks. Since such hard training can lower your hemoglobin value and cause other problems, you should avoid all-out anaerobic training until just before you need it. You have some of the chemical capacity for going into oxygen debt simply by being alive and healthy. Even the most poorly trained person can sprint a short distance. You develop much more of it during your aerobic training. If you do speed training that takes you beyond your aerobic capacity you are also doing anaerobic training, and for most sports that is enough. Not everybody has the determination to train like Roger Craig, nor could many people stand it.

Roger Craig, NFL offensive player of the year in 1988, trained hard: In the spring of 1988, he rose at 6:30 AM to run 4 to 8 miles on a hilly course at a seven-minute mile pace uphill and under six-minute downhill, three days a week—excellent aerobic training. Continuing to train like a track runner, he ran on the track on three other days. He did fifteen sprints of 100 yards, then ran 220 sprints with thirty seconds of rest between each— probably more than enough anaerobic training.

Glycogen is fuel, and each of your muscles stores a supply of it. When you run out of glycogen, usually after more than two hours of competition, you are dependent upon blood sugar, and most of your energy will come from burning fat. This is not as efficient as burning carbohydrates, so you cannot move as fast. Even worse, your central nervous system feeds on carbohydrates, so when you run short of glycogen your skills in any sport begin to fail.

To increase your glycogen supply, you should begin by increasing your capacity. That is done by exhausting your supply. If you train or compete until you run short of glycogen, as in running twenty miles, your capacity will increase. Then you need to fill your capacity by eating carbohydrates—which is why marathon runners eat so much pasta before a race—and by resting. You should abstain from glycogen-burning activity for at least two days after depleting your supply to allow your tank to fill.

The last aid to endurance has been discussed under strength. A weak muscle has to work harder than a strong muscle to do the same job, thus requiring more fuel and oxygen.

Most sports are not considered endurance sports, but in most it is possible to become tired enough to lose your skill. Don't let it happen to you.

## SKILLS

In many sports, training your skills is even more important than training for strength, speed, or endurance. If it came down to hitting a wedge shot close to the pin, you'd pick a skilled golfer over the most highly conditioned marathon runner or tennis champion.

Skill is what you need to shoot a basket, hit a backhand, complete a pass, bunt a baseball, or kick a goal. Each sport requires special skills, although some, like golf, depend almost entirely upon skills. In any case, you cannot succeed in sports without developing certain skills. To learn how to go about it, first learn something about your body.

One of the great wonders of your body is something we might call your Control System, a combination of at least four neuromuscular skills: Kinesthesia is your sense of the position of your body. You know, without seeing, the location of each part. Coordination is your remarkable ability to use your nerves to control exact movements of your muscles, whether it is the tiny but complicated movements of writing your name or the large yet complex movement of swinging a bat to hit a fast-moving ball. Memory is what you need to perform coordinated movements exactly, time after time. Reflexes are like commands given by some unseen being; before you have time to think, your reflex puts into motion your correct action, such as balancing on a bicycle.

Your Control System is what performed the almost magical feat of learning to ride a bicycle. Somehow it discarded all your clumsy movements and retained only those that allowed you to regain your balance before your conscious mind even knew you were losing it. Nobody knows exactly how this works, but they know you can learn almost any skill if you use your Control System properly.

The simplest way to train your Control System is to give it a goal. For example, think about throwing a Frisbee. If you did not have the goal of throwing it straight, you would not care how much it curved. But if you want to learn to throw it straight, then any other throw is rejected and not remembered by your Control

System. In other words, give yourself a goal and your Control System will, by trial and error, gradually approach perfection.

There is one serious fault with this trial-and-error method: your goal may not be the correct one. A tennis player teaching himself may be satisfied with the goal of returning every backhand. As a beginner it is more satisfying to return 95 percent of your backhands, even though they are slow and short, than it is to hit crisp returns but miss half of them. Your problem is that after a year or so of success against other beginners, you find that your steady backhand is too weak and your opponents pound it past you. The worst part is that your Control System has learned it, and now you have to unlearn it before you can learn a more correct backhand.

The most important lesson you can learn about acquiring a skill is: LEARN IT RIGHT. It can be fun learning a skill all by yourself. Often an inferior form is easier and faster to learn, so your initial success comes more quickly. But a second- or third-best method will limit you, and sometime in the future you will regret taking the easiest path.

Therefore, the goal you give your Control System should be a clear picture of the best way to perform a skill. Here are six ways to do it:

A coach can teach you the most, especially if you are young. A really good coach can set your goals, helping your Control System correct your errors while at the same time inspiring you to learn more.

If you observe good form, your Control System can use it as your goal. Watch good players in the stadium or on television. Use a VCR to collect action pictures of good form and study the technique, in slow motion if possible. To become an expert on technique, you begin by observing, but you must study what you observe.

You should read as part of your study of technique. Books or magazines can tell you why one technique is best and make you aware of small movements that you might miss in your observations. Words, along with pictures, can give you a mental blueprint and thus give your Control System a clear goal.

Think about your form. If you never think about it, how do you expect to know when it goes wrong? Thought is the bridge between information in the form of words or pictures and the final command to your Control System.

You begin to think when you try to figure out why a certain technique is better than another. You may see all the good tennis players bend their front knee while making a stroke, but it feels more comfortable to you to stand up straight. If you think enough to realize that your knee should be bent to allow your weight to move forward as you stroke, then your Control System will accept your command to bend your knee.

Even more important than bridging the gap between your observation and your command, thinking can give you answers. If you have a problem and cannot find the answer in a book or from your coach or on film, sometimes you can think it out. An example might be your golf swing. Suppose you are slicing your drives. You can think of the cause: The ball is spinning clockwise because you are swinging from the outside in and pulling your driver across the ball. You think and experiment until you learn that tucking your right elbow closer to your body before your downswing will correct the spin. That small inch or two would not show in a picture, but you could discover it by thinking.

You can find most answers with common-sense physics, but you don't have to study physics. You do have to study every movement involved in every skill you want to learn. Go through the movement in your mind in slow motion, and think about each part of your body that has anything at all to do with the skill, including those parts you want to keep out of the way and relaxed. The more you study the skill, the more you will understand the best way to do it.

Another method of sending correct commands to your Control System is by feeling. Once in a while, during practice or play, you will make a movement that feels exactly right. When you do, you should point this out to your Control System. Tell it, "That's the way I want to do it every time." It usually surprises an athlete to get a perfect result with so little effort, but that is the way perfection feels. When it happens, try to use it again.

You can also send messages to your Control System by imagining. It is easier if you have experienced the perfect movement, but if not, you can certainly imagine the perfect result. Scientific experiments have proved that people can improve at shooting free throws or throwing darts with no other practice but their imagination.

The reason behind such magic is the fact that your Control System does not know whether the picture it receives is real or imaginary. Your body can react with all the symptoms of fright when you see a figure hiding in the shadows ahead, whether the figure is a mugger or a tree stump. Your unconscious mechanism reacts the same way in either case.

Ben Hogan, one of the greatest golfers of all time, saw every shot in his imagination before he hit the ball, trying to "feel" the shot. He was telling his Control System what to do.

Now you have a toolbox full of methods for teaching your Control System, but they are not enough to make you skillful. The one activity that will make you great is correct practice.

Most people and many athletes think that practice means nothing more than trying to perform the skill you want to learn. In reality, practice can be divided into four different kinds.

First you practice to learn your skill. You use one or all of the methods for teaching your Control System what to do, and you work at it until you can do it correctly. That includes selecting the right way to do each part of it and putting the parts together into the whole movement. In the tennis forehand, for example, you learn the grip, the footwork, the backswing, timing of your stroke, and the follow-through. Once you can do each of those correctly, put them together and work on the whole stroke.

Next, after learning to perform the whole stroke reasonably well, you practice to perfect it. That means drill. You must do it over and over again until you can do it almost perfectly, doing it the same way each time. Some skills may require thousands of hours of drill. Too many athletes never perfect their skills because they cannot stand the drudgery of constant drill.

If you know you need more drilling but you dislike the chore, there are ways to make it more interesting. Practicing with others is usually more fun, and you might think about finding the most pleasant place to practice. Concentration makes anything more interesting, and one of the best ways to concentrate is to make your practice competitive. Compete against yourself. Keep records of your progress and keep trying to break your record. And use variety by stopping one drill when you seem to have it right and starting on another skill.

Third, after you are satisfied, you practice for the purpose of retaining your skill. That does not take much time compared with your drilling stage. A few minutes twice a week should retain most skills, or perhaps competition is all the refresher you need. It is up to you to decide, based on your results.

Your fourth and last type of practice is during competition. It would be foolish to practice during an important match, but in practice matches, unimportant games, or competition where you can win easily, you should practice.

Competitive practice is different because your opponent is trying to beat you, whereas in ordinary practice someone is working with you. For example, in tennis practice the ball is hit where you expect it to be, but in a match your opponent is trying to do exactly the opposite. Therefore, instead of practicing your forehand on a waist-high shot with your feet perfectly positioned, you get a low twister that you have to hit on the run. You have learned the basic stroke, but difficult shots require adjustments, so competitive practice means experimenting with the right kind of adjustment for an unusual situation. If you are only trying to win, you can return the difficult shot as safely as possible, but to practice you should try to hit it well. In other words, use a less desirable technique that needs practice instead of the one most likely to win.

A striking example of the difference between competition in a game and drill is seen in basketball foul shooting. Among top basketball players, anyone who sinks more than 80 percent of free throws is considered a good foul shooter. And yet an obscure player named Ted St. Martin set a world record for free throws by sinking 927 in a row. There should not be that much difference simply because you are in the midst of a game. This is an area where anybody, especially the highly paid pros, should be able to improve immensely.

Possibly the most important consideration about skills is to learn correctly. Players who learn incorrectly almost always develop flaws. You can see flaws in professional players who succeed in spite of them, but how much better could they be if they didn't have those flaws? If you take pains to learn correctly from the start, you will save yourself much pain later on. Perhaps you'll even save your career.

# 6

# Program Your Brain to Win

When you have chosen the sport best suited to your natural talents, improved your condition as much as possible, and learned all the skills you can, are you as good an athlete as you'll ever be?

The answer is, "No!" Even if your racing car is the best in the race, you won't win with a poor driver. In an athletic competition your well-prepared body is like the car and your brain is like the driver. You need to have finely tuned mental control to be the best possible athlete.

Mental control is complicated, and if you leave it to chance it can be more than difficult: it can turn against you. You can try to simplify it and gain some control by dividing it into planning, emotional control, and concentration.

## PLANNING

While you are competing you do not have time for careful thinking. Therefore, you should do as much planning as possible before the game begins. Make your plans calmly and objectively for every possible situation, and have them ready to put into action when each situation arises.

Your Control System will automatically execute each plan if you have told it exactly what to do. Indecision can cause you to use the wrong tool or use the right tool improperly. For example, when your tennis opponent hits a short shot from the base line, you run for it and barely reach it. You have a choice of at least six shots to try, but you can't consider them all in your desperate rush to reach the ball. If you have made a decision beforehand to use an angled drop shot in this situation you will do it without thinking. If you try to think while moving for the ball, you will probably try something else or even compromise with a weak tap back to your opponent.

Give your Control System exact orders. It cannot make decisions.

Begin your planning by collecting information. First you need information about yourself. You need to know all your strengths and weaknesses so that your plan favors your strengths. You need to know your capabilities. What is your percentage for each kind of shot? What will happen to you if you run the first ten miles of a marathon at a three-minute mile pace? Can you block a linebacker with a knee-high dive? You need this complete information about yourself in order to form your basic plan.

Your basic plan is what you will do under average circumstances if your opponents perform in the usual way. Thus, a tennis player might choose a hard, deep shot down the line as his normal forehand, ready to change it only for some good reason.

Next you need information about the site of your competition. The site does not change in bowling, but every golf course is different. Include the weather in this, because your tactics may have to change in rain or cold.

Information about your opponent is vital to planning for a boxing match, tennis, racing, or team sports. The top teams obtain scouting reports containing detailed information about their opponents, but as an individual you may have to find your own information. In order of importance, you can obtain information from: films, playing against your opponent, watching your opponent, scouting reports, written accounts of competition, and watching opponents warm up.

Use all your information to form your plan. Start with your basic plan and change it to fit the site of the event and your opponents.

As soon as your plan is ready, begin to make alternate plans. You need an alternate plan in case the weather changes. You want an alternate plan for any change in tactics by your opponent. You must be ready to change plans if any of your skills fail.

When you have a complete set of alternate plans, you should begin your visualization. That means you imagine yourself in each situation and "see" yourself carrying out your plan. In this way you tell your Control System what to do no matter what happens. In the 1968 Olympics, Al Oerter won his fourth Olympic gold medal in the discus when rain surprised the throwers. The others threw poorly, but Oerter threw better than ever because he had a plan for rain. He said, "I know ahead of time what I will do under every condition."

Jack Nicklaus, golf's greatest winner, outlined his visualization technique: "I never hit a shot, even in practice, without having a very sharp in-focus picture of it in my head. It's like a color movie. First, I 'see' the ball where I want it to finish. Then the scene quickly changes and I 'see' the ball going there. Then there's a sort of fade-out, and the next scene shows me making the kind of swing that will turn the previous images into reality."

You should have at least one alternate plan ready to avoid failure because of fatigue. Your plan should allow for pacing yourself over long contests, for using tactics that will shorten the time, for replenishing your glycogen supply by consuming glucose, and for making the proper changes when fatigue causes your skills to diminish.

## EMOTIONAL CONTROL

Why do you suppose a football coach gives his team a stirring talk before the game? Why does a coach put a newspaper clipping on the bulletin board quoting some derogatory remark by an opponent?

The purpose is to excite the team. Excited players have more adrenaline flowing and are motivated to play harder. They ignore pain and fatigue. Football history is full of "fired-up" teams that have upset highly favored teams. Some of these great upsets are viewed as miracles, like that of a frail woman who lifted a car to free a child trapped under the wreckage.

University of Texas coach Darrell Royal said, "Only angry people win football games." And sportswriter Paul Gallico said, "Cruelty and absolute lack of mercy are essential qualities in every successful prizefighter."

Athletes often try to "psych" themselves. They try to bring themselves to a state of excitement where they seem stronger and faster and more aggressive.

One way to do this is by using your emotions as energy. Whenever you feel an emotion, you have energy to go along with it. If you can learn to use that energy, you will have a source of extra power.

As an example, Russian athletes are given autoconditioning training to help them "choose their moods and thoughts at will," according to Grigori Raiport, president of the Russian Success Method. Raiport was trained in futuristic sports techniques at the Moscow National Research Institute of Physical Culture. When inspired, Raiport says, athletes could feel "a tingling in the jaw, coolness in the temples, lightness in the body." He says that the Russians would have managed speed skater Dan Jansen properly. Jansen's sister died on the day he was to compete in the 1988 Winter Olympics. U.S. officials left him alone in his grief, and Jansen fell during his race. Raiport says, "Russians would have handled the tragedy differently. Realizing that any strong emotion possesses energy, they would have tried to transform the negative energy of grief into a constructive force. Instead of leaving Dan alone, they would have been with him all day, saying: "You're going to do this for your sister. Imagine that she is watching you, that she is waiting for you at the finish line.""

In sports where "hustle" can win, such added energy is beneficial. But when you use skills requiring accuracy, you do best when you are relaxed. It is possible to be fired up and still be relaxed in the muscles necessary for your skill movements, but it is highly unlikely. Under the influence of excitement, a basketball player may dive into the crowd to save a ball headed out of bounds, but that same excitement may cause him to shoot poorly compared with his relaxed shots.

Relaxation is the opposite of tension, and tension is the primary cause of skill failure. Any emotion that causes tension, especially fear, will harm your skills. The great former football coach Tom Landry said, "I don't believe you can be emotional and concentrate the way you must to be effective."

Once your skill is learned, your Control System executes it as well as you have learned it. Your skill will fail only if you interfere with your Control System.

One way to interfere is by thinking too hard about your action while you do it. A novice artist tries to draw a line by concentrating hard and guiding each small movement of the brush. A good artist draws that same line with one quick, light stroke. The first draws crabbed, inaccurate lines, whereas the second draws straight and accurate lines. A relaxed and easy movement is ultimately more accurate and skillful.

Thus, the tension that causes poor performance can come from the tension of trying too hard or from the tension caused by emotion. Therefore, you should psych yourself up to an excited pitch only when accuracy is not necessary. A football lineman needs as much hustle as possible and less accuracy. A golfer needs exactly the opposite. It all depends upon the specific requirements of your sport and especially the particular situation.

It would be great if you could push one button to fire yourself up for maximum performance and push another button to bring on the perfect relaxation you need for maximum accuracy. You can't do it with buttons, but it is possible to approach such an ideal condition.

In a situation when you want to psych yourself into an excited state of all-out effort, you might think of your mind as the jockey and your body as the horse. You need a psychological "whip" to excite yourself.

Your whip can be anything, as long as it works. Most athletes talk to themselves, silently or aloud. Some athletes berate themselves with scornful criticism when they do something wrong. That is not a good idea because your Control System does not function properly under negative input.

A whip can be a "carrot" or a "stick." The carrot is incentive—something you want. The stick is punishment you want to escape by doing the right thing. If you use the stick, you are making a threat, and such negative input will cause tension and reduce your skills. You will succeed far more often with the carrot. Give yourself an incentive that makes you excited about winning.

You can imagine yourself winning. Imagine the cheers of the crowd and the approval of your friends. Imagine receiving all the rewards of winning. Imagine seeing your name in headlines or being interviewed for television. Use your mind to give you reasons to play with great emotion and hustle.

But what if your situation calls for a calm, relaxed approach? Obviously, you cannot relax if you feel fear, worry, or anxiety. Nor can your Control System make a skillful movement if you try to guide yourself through it, slowly and carefully concentrating on each muscle. Once your Control System has learned a skill, you can only give it the order and let it take over completely.

If you do not completely believe this, try typing or playing the piano while thinking about each finger position. Or try riding a bicycle while consciously correcting every tiny imbalance with a movement of the front wheel. Your Control System has a shortcut to your nerves and muscles. It can do the job far faster and more accurately than you can do with your conscious mind.

Use your conscious mind to decide. Do you want to shoot for the basket or pass off to a teammate? Hit the tennis ball down the line or crosscourt? Plunge straight toward the tackler or try to sidestep? But once you have made the decision, let your Control System handle it. Never send your Control System any kind of message in the midst of a movement.

Thus, any kind of interruption may cause your Control System to send the wrong message. It can be a conscious thought at the wrong time, or it can be an emotion that causes tension in one or more of the muscles you need to make a skillful movement. To relax, you must shut out those emotions.

You cannot shut out emotions simply by using your willpower and saying, "I won't fear anything." That's like telling yourself you won't think of a white elephant. The harder you try, the more you will find a white elephant slipping into your thoughts. You cannot do it negatively. The only way you can eliminate one thought is by substituting a more interesting thought, one that involves your mind so much that you don't think of anything else. It is like eliminating a small pain by inflicting a greater pain. The best way to eliminate negative thoughts or feelings is to have a strong positive thought or feeling.

*The Power of Positive Thinking*, by Norman Vincent Peale, dealt with this subject and its effect on your whole life. It is not easy to think positively all the time, but you should start trying to learn how, whatever your age.

The rewards of positive thinking can be great. One of the best examples of positive thinking in sports happened on the seventeenth green at Pebble Beach, during the last round of the 1982 U.S. Open. Tom Watson was tied with Jack Nicklaus, who had already finished. Watson's tee shot on the seventeenth left him in the tall grass above the slick and sloping green. Watching on television, Nicklaus felt certain that Watson would not be able to stop the ball on his second shot close enough to sink the putt for a par. Watson's caddy pleaded, "Get it close."

Almost any golfer, even most of the pros, would concentrate on getting it close, fearing the ball would run on past by several feet. But Watson is different. He thinks positively. He told his caddy, "I'm going to sink it."

He studied the frightening situation once more, took his stance, and swung his club delicately. The ball popped out of the grass, rolled down the green, and dropped into the cup.

Bill Rogers, playing with Watson, called it "a thousand to one shot." Nicklaus was shocked. And once again, many people called Watson "the luckiest golfer alive."

But Watson has done it too many times for it to be nothing more than luck. He had already holed out from off the putting surface on the tenth and fourteenth holes! His positive attitude eliminates the tension that would bring about the shots other golfers fear. When he thought, "I'm going to sink it," he gave himself two advantages over his opponents.

First, he gave himself a target. He visualized the ball rolling into the cup, whereas others only visualized it stopping close to the cup. They usually hit their much easier target, but Watson sometimes hits his.

Second, Watson does not allow negative thoughts to block his Control System. He has invested countless hours of practice in teaching his Control System to do what he wants to do, and he does not prevent his Control System from working efficiently by tensing his muscles because of fear or other negative thoughts.

You should start thinking positive thoughts. One of your most important goals should be to give yourself the right philosophy about losing. Keep in mind that there are far more losers than winners in sports. Even the best professionals lose some of the time. Babe Ruth struck out far more often than he hit a home run. Losing is a fact of life in sports. If you are emotionally upset to a great degree every time you lose, perhaps a career in sports is not for you.

If you enjoy competition, if you like to improve your skills and make progress, if you can be proud of yourself for doing your best even though you lose, then you are on the right track toward emotional control.

If you can stand over a ten-foot putt and think, "I have everything to gain by sinking this putt, and really nothing to lose," you set yourself up for a pleasant bonus if you sink it and you avoid the childish, "crybaby" feeling so many athletes show. But if you think, "I'll lose if I miss this putt," you set yourself up for unhappiness, not only at that moment but throughout most of your sports career. What's worse, that negative thought will cause you to miss many putts. You should regard winning as something nice happening to you, not something that is your just due.

Psychologists name two attitudes that can ruin an athletic career. "Fear of failure" is obvious. If winning becomes so important to you that you cannot tolerate losing, then your fear of losing will cause you to lose. The other attitude is not so obvious. "Fear of winning" harms many athletes. They block themselves from winning because then they will be expected to win again and they don't believe they can. In either case they fail because fear tightens their muscles at the wrong time.

Byron Nelson, one of the all-time great golfers, said, "Putting affects the nerves more than anything. I would actually get nauseated over three-footers, and there were tournaments when I couldn't keep a meal down for four days."

Your best emotional control is to have no emotion at all. If you give your Control System a command calmly and remain calm while it is carried out, you will perform as well as you do in practice. In fact, your Control System can help you stay calm!

You can learn to make physical relaxation automatic. That is hard to believe, but think about biofeedback. Scientists have proved, and many people have demonstrated to themselves, that people can control even their involuntary muscles. One of the easiest tests proving this involves the temperature of your fingers. A thermometer is attached to a finger to show the temperature. By thinking the right thoughts, you can raise or lower the temperature of your fingers. You can also relax the tension in your "frown" muscles, reduce or eliminate the pain from a migraine headache, lower your blood pressure, and a number of other feats that seem like miracles.

One of your most important long-range goals, beneficial in areas other than sports, should be to learn relaxation.

You can learn relaxation in four steps:

1. Learn the feeling of tension.
2. Learn to relax that tension consciously.
3. Learn to relax muscles while other muscles are in action.
4. Teach your Control System to begin that relaxation automatically, even when you are not conscious of it.

You can begin learning the feeling of tension by clenching your fist as hard as possible. That feeling is tension. Put your thumb and forefingers on opposite sides of your forearm. Feel how it tightens when you clench your fist.

Now practice relaxing tense muscles. Put your thumb on your biceps and your fingers on the back of your arm, feeling your triceps. When you clench your fist, you probably tighten both your biceps and your triceps. Now put the back of your hand on a table or on your knee and push down as hard as you can. The muscles on the back of your arm, your triceps, must tighten to force your forearm down, but your biceps probably tightened as well. Practice relaxing your biceps while tightening your triceps. Then put your hand under the table or under your leg and lift. Your triceps should be relaxed while your biceps are tight. Now clench your fist while both of those muscles are relaxed. When you can relax antagonistic muscles or unneeded muscles, you have learned the difference between tension and relaxation.

The third step is harder, mainly because it is more difficult to detect tension when there is movement. Start with clenching and unclenching your fist. Even though you have learned how to clench without tightening your biceps and triceps, you probably feel a little tightening in at least one of your triceps when you clench and unclench rapidly. Notice that you can control this rather easily when you think about it. Now try the same principle with one of your skill motions.

For example, a tennis player might swing a forehand stroke. Try to feel all the unnecessary muscles that tighten when you stroke. These unnecessary muscles may be in your legs, in your other arm, in your neck and torso, or even in the arm you use. Are you tightening your biceps or triceps when you don't need to? This self-examination can take a lot of time and effort, but every unnecessary muscle you are able to relax will improve your skill.

Sometimes, while you are practicing your skills, concentrate on relaxing unnecessary muscles. You won't conquer these bad habits in one day, but you will soon learn to relax unnecessary muscles while you are in action.

Now comes the fourth and final step. Up to this point it has been as if you pushed a button to correct something you notice. Now you want to teach your Control System to push that button automatically. Your goal is to train your Control System to notice any unwanted tension and relax it.

Any muscle control you can do consciously is possible to do automatically. You teach your Control System through feelings in your muscles and through conscious thoughts or commands. You combine them by noticing proper relaxation and calling it to the attention of your Control System. You also call attention to it by noticing each time it fails. When you learned to ride a bicycle, your goal was to ride straight. Each fall was wrong, so your Control System discarded it. Show your Control System your goal by relaxing all unneeded muscles consciously. Slowly but surely, your Control System will zero in on that goal until finally you won't have to think about it at all.

Even after your Control System has learned automatic relaxation, it is possible for you to override it by feeling a strong emotion that produces tension. It is not as easy to practice relaxation under emotional tension because you first have to produce that emotion. The best way to do it is to wait until you feel the emotion or tension, then consciously relax and tell your Control System that that is what you want it to do. Some athletes try to simulate emotional situations while practicing by saying something like, "I have this putt for the Masters Championship." Lee Trevino did it unconsciously when he was young by betting on putting contests. "You don't know what pressure is until you play for five bucks with only two in your pocket."

You can also practice relaxation when you feel a strong emotion caused by something entirely different. There is no certain way to practice while tense, so you must try anything you can think of, especially during competition.

If you can teach your Control System to eliminate tension from your skill movements even when your natural inclination should leave you tense with fear, you will give yourself what may be the single most powerful competitive tool any athlete can have.

## CONCENTRATION

Concentration means giving your attention to only one thing. If your concentration is on the right thing, it is of great value to you in sports and most other activities.

A six-year-old boy was trying to shoot baskets but missing more than he made. His coach told him about concentration. The boy squinted his eyes and took his time, and he made ten in a row.

Bill Bradley, one of the great pro basketball shooters, always concentrated on the front of the rim. No matter where his body was moving, his eyes were anchored to the rim. It is the simplest and most precise way to point out your goal to your Control System.

You concentrate on different things during different sports and at different times during the same sport. In tennis, you watch the ball as it comes toward you and concentrate on meeting it at exactly the right spot. Immediately, your concentration changes to powering and guiding the ball with a strong follow-through. Then you concentrate on your opponent to learn as quickly as possible what kind of shot hc or she will make. Once the ball leaves your opponent's racket, you concentrate again on the ball. Any lapse in your concentration can cause an error or a less-than-perfect shot. And after the point ends, you concentrate on something else, perhaps tactics or an analysis of your last point.

Think about the action in your sport. Decide where your concentration should be in each part:

Do you have a target? If so, your concentration should be on that target—the ball, if it is moving, or the exact point you want it to go in basketball, bowling, pitching, passing, hockey, or soccer. If your target is an opponent—as in football or boxing—concentrate on the part of him or her you want to reach. During the movement, that should be your only concentration.

As soon as you finish that movement, concentrate on preparation for the next one. In a sport like boxing, this is immediate. In sports like golf and bowling, you have time to think. Intense concentration on your opponent allows you to anticipate his next move. Therefore, in tennis you concentrate on your opponent's body position and backswing in order to gain a step or two on the shot.

Between plays, switch your concentration to sending positive pictures and commands to your Control System so as to have full control over your emotions. If you let your mind wander between plays, you have little control. This should be the last thing you do before play continues. If you have extra time, you can begin by concentrating on tactics. Are you following your plan? If so, and it is not working, should you change tactics?

Don't make the mistake many athletes make of berating themselves for their mistakes in judgment or errors of execution. Be as positive as you possibly can. Tell yourself something to do, not something not to do. You would be wise to memorize a checklist so that it comes into your mind whenever you need it, especially when you are tired or caught up emotionally in the competition. Your brain does not function well under the stress of competition, and you can help it in this way. Keep your list simple:

- Am I watching the ball (target)?
- Am I hustling?
- Am I sending only positive pictures to my
  Control System?
- Am I using the right tactics?
- Is each of my skills functioning well?
- Am I pacing myself in order to keep playing at
  my best?

If you work on mental control by making plans, by learning a positive attitude, and by concentrating on the right thought at the right time, you will make the most of your natural talents and your training. If you are serious about your sport, you would be foolish to do any less.

# Be Your Own Director

You know something about training and competing, but there is more. Most amateur athletes drift along, doing their best as competitors but leaving many important details to their parents, to their coaches, or to chance. You can use the following list to remind yourself not to neglect these important duties.

## STUDY

You need to study even if you think sports are the only thing worth your hard work. Do you want to be eligible to compete for your school teams? At the very minimum you must study enough to win passing grades. Do you want to work at some nonplaying job in pro sports? Obviously, you must learn enough to qualify. Have you considered what you will do after your sports career? Unless you amass a small fortune as an athlete and have no other ambition in life, you will want to work at something when your pro sports career ends between the ages of twenty-five and forty. Why not do most of your studying before you retire?

## USE ALL THE HELP YOU CAN GET

Only a superhuman could think of succeeding in sports without any help from others. You need help from your parents, coaches, friends, and many others.

If your parents are not behind you, your sports career will be difficult, if not impossible. Many parents forbid their children to play sports in which injuries are common. Some parents consider sports a waste of time. Some parents have preconceived notions about which sport their children should play. Some parents make plans for their children that do not include practice.

You need to sell yourself as an athlete. If your behavior is good, your parents will have no reason to punish you by depriving you of time for sports. If your grades are good, they can't say you have to study instead. You should talk with them, letting them know how important sports are to you. Do what you can to get them behind you to the point that they encourage you rather than hinder you. In the worst possible situation, ask your coach to help influence your parents.

Your coach is of great importance. Many young athletes look up to their coaches as parental figures, receiving and accepting more and better advice than from negligent parents. But before you put yourself in his or her hands entirely, you should evaluate your coach.

A coach is a teacher. He or she teaches you how to play your sport. As a beginner you won't be able to judge your coach fully as a teacher, but you should be aware that some high school coaches are academic teachers not fully prepared to be coaches. If your coach is unable to help you learn, you should try to learn from somebody else without jeopardizing your place on the team. Sometimes you can find a former athlete or even another coach to help you. Or you might help yourself by reading or watching films.

A coach may be bad because he is overcritical instead of encouraging, or because he advocates winning by cheating, or because he plays favorites, or risks injuries. Supportive parents may be able to help you in such cases. In an extreme case, you might be wise to take up another sport.

Whether your coach is great or poor, you should still study your sport. You should do all you can to become an expert—in each of the skills you need to know, in tactics, in psychology, in mental control, in everything that might give you the slightest edge.

The most important step in learning anything is to want to learn. If you really want to learn, you will read. You will listen to your coach and other players. You will watch games, live or on television, and study every move. You will ask questions and look for extra coaching. Most of all you will think. Ask yourself *why*. Why is it better to bend your front knee in a tennis stroke? Why do you try to see the ball strike your bat in baseball? Why is the position of your right elbow important in your golf swing?

The more you want to learn, the more you will study and the more you will improve. And the more you learn, the better you will play.

To help yourself want to learn, you might start by setting goals.

Goals should be serious. Don't set a goal you do not intend to reach, because then you may form the habit of ignoring goals whenever it is easier to do so. Be careful about changing goals; don't change just because the new one is easier to reach.

Goals should include long-range goals and short-range goals, arranged so that the short-range are stepping stones toward your ultimate goals. Enjoy your success each time you reach another goal.

Goals should be recorded. If you write a goal down, it is easier to remember and it will constantly remind you to go after it. If you tell somebody else your goal, you will have extra incentive to strive for it.

Use a set of goals to guide you and to motivate you.

## CONTROL YOUR LIFESTYLE

Sometimes athletes will go too far to reach their goals. It's easy to want something so badly that you would be willing to do anything to get it, but when you want a career in pro sports, steroids are not the way to obtain that dream. Nobody with any common sense would risk bodily harm, loss of playing ability, expulsion from the sport, a prison sentence, or death for a few moments of glory.

Some people may tell you that steroids will make you stronger and faster, and that they won't do any harm. You may even believe that steroids will give you an edge. Before you make any decisions concerning steroids, here are the facts:

**Don't mess with Mother Nature.** Anabolic steroids are synthetic hormones. Natural hormones are produced by your body to excite you for specific purposes. Examples are the fight-or-flight reaction, the result of adrenaline, and sexual arousal, the result of sex hormones. Synthetic hormones produce unnatural reactions in your body that interfere with your natural reactions. Athletes should be wary of putting anything foreign into their bodies, whether it is drugs, cigarettes, alcohol, or steroids. If you are a male, steroids can produce acne, make you bald, develop your breasts, and shrivel your testicles so that you cannot become a father. If you are female, you risk masculinization—loss of hair on your head, growth of a beard, shrunken breasts, abnormal genital growth, and a deep voice. A study published in the *Journal of the American Medical Association* estimates that half a million American high school seniors take steroids, with a third of them beginning by the age of fifteen. For young athletes, taking steroids can halt their growth before they reach their full height.

One of Russia's female Olympic athletes who used steroids said, "My whole hormonal system is destroyed, my health is ruined . . . and my life is still ahead of me. I would have liked to become a mother."

**Steroids can be hazardous to your health.** You might develop cancer of the liver, hepatitis, and leukemia. You might suffer kidney failure or heart attacks. Glen Maur, former champion bodybuilder, had a heart attack at the age of thirty-three from steroid use. David Jenkins, an Olympic silver medalist in 1972, who is now convicted of directing an international steroid smuggling operation, says, "There is the potential for fatal results and that's the scary thing, so what you're dealing with is a loaded gun." John Kordic, a twenty-seven-year-old hockey player in the NHL, died in 1994 from excessive anabolic steroid use.

**Steroids can ruin your personality.** This effect is called "roid rage" because it is caused by steroids. It makes you anxious, hostile, and violently aggressive, and it makes you do things you normally wouldn't do. In a story in *Sports Illustrated*, Tommy Chaikin, a four-year football letterman at South Carolina, tells how steroids made him violent and caused such extreme anxiety attacks that he almost committed suicide. "I was sitting in my room . . . with the barrel of a loaded

0.357 Magnum pressed under my chin. It had all come down from the steroids, the crap I'd taken to get big and strong and aggressive so I could play this game that I love."

**Steroid use is against the law.** Steroids are illegal without a prescription. Olympic sports regulations require testing of participants, and all users are banned. Ben Johnson, who won the 1988 Olympic 100-meter race in world-record time, tested positive for a banned substance. He lost his gold medal and his world record, he was banned for two years (and thus lost more than a million dollars worth of advertising contracts), and he went home in disgrace. Other sports are following suit and testing their athletes, including the National Football League.

**It hurts your conscience and your sense of yourself.** If you like yourself, you don't want to think of yourself as a cheater. You'll take more pride in yourself if you can play well without artificial aid.

**It's costly, in more ways than one.** If you buy steroids on the black market, you can't be sure you are getting what you are paying for. David Jenkins says, "We came to the conclusion that out of about every 20 purchases of steroids carried out in a gym or on the black market, probably 19 of those would be counterfeit in some form [not the steroids the dealer claimed they were]." You can buy high-quality American steroids, but you need a prescription and money. A single injection can cost as much as $300, while pills can cost as much as $175 a month.

**The odds are against you.** Many people have gained weight and strength from steroids, but only a few have achieved great athletic success, and most of those athletes end up paying a price for it in the future. Most athletes have been successful without using steroids. If you continue training hard and striving toward your goals, you will have a better chance of becoming successful than you will by taking a few pills that might give you strength but end up damaging or killing you later.

This choice—immediate gratification vs. future success—may be very difficult for you to make, especially if you are young. Steroids can be very tempting. But the sooner you begin to make choices favoring your future, the sooner you'll have a future favoring you. Before you make any decisions, think about the pros and cons of that decision. Think not only about how your decision will affect you now, but also about how it will affect you in the future.

The National College Athletic Association (NCAA) is becoming more strict. You are now required to sign a consent form for drug testing early in each academic year. If you test positive, you will lose a year of competition. Even the use of tobacco products is prohibited during practice and competition.

Your choice of lifestyle may well be the biggest choice you'll ever make.

## SPECIALIZATION

If you start high school with several sports on your schedule, the time will come when you must make a decision to specialize. Let's say you are an all-round athlete in junior high. You are the running back on the football team, forward on the basketball team, and in the spring you are center fielder on the baseball team and a sprinter on the track team. You are good in golf and tennis and play some soccer when you have time.

You also like to play racquetball and to bowl, and you'd like to try other sports. Obviously, you have to cut down on some of those and focus on a few if you want to excel in any of them.

It would be easy for you to go out for football, basketball, and baseball in high school because each has a different season. You could play golf and tennis on weekends and in the summer. If you had any energy left, you could fit in an occasional evening of bowling or racquetball. But even if you were good enough to play all those sports, there are drawbacks to trying to pack all of them into your schedule.

First, such a schedule would leave little time for other activities. You will not have time for homework and studying or your friends. You will have to spend all your time and focus all your energy on sports. Second, you would have no time for out-of-season training. Such training is important if you want to achieve success. For instance, a basketball player must practice all year to be a star. Third, you would probably go stale from constant training and competition. Rest is an important ingredient in preparing to compete, and you would have no rest.

On the other hand, you need to consider carefully which sports to cut out so that you don't eliminate your best chance for the future. For example, you may be a basketball star now and so you eliminate soccer. But if you only grow to be 5'11" tall your chances are slim in college and pro basketball. Or you may have been playing baseball since you were eight while you began tennis only last year. How can you judge your relative ability with only one year's experience against six or seven years?

This is a real problem, but it may not be as difficult as it seems. For one reason, even though you like to play several sports, you are probably not equally good in all sports.

Most athletes are college scholarship material in no more than one sport. You should be able to identify that sport during your junior year of high school. Then you can devote all your training time to that one sport. It will help you develop much faster than if you play it only during the season. Here again, it is a balance between present enjoyment and your future. If you love basketball but are serious about a future in baseball, you can play basketball in intramural or pick-up games but concentrate primarily on developing your baseball skills.

It will be easy enough for you to concentrate on your main sport and still participate in other sports for fun. Your goal is to improve as much as possible in your main sport. And you should expect to do so for at least a year before you can earn a scholarship. Great success in sports, as in most things, comes to those who give it close to 100 percent in terms of effort. You cannot keep up with other athletes if you only devote 25 percent of your year's effort to one sport. Sooner or later you must specialize, and it should be no later than your senior year of high school if you hope to excel at the next level.

## Pursue a Scholarship

For almost every good high school athlete, one of the most important goals is to earn a college scholarship. If you are offered an athletic scholarship, it means somebody thinks enough of your prospects to give you room, board, books, and fees worth about $5,000 a year, plus tuition worth anywhere from $1,500 at a state university to $15,000 at a private college or university.

The money and prestige involved make it worth your efforts, which means you should do more than merely play well.

Before you begin to think seriously about a scholarship, you should know something about the general situation. More than 3,000 colleges in the United States are divided into four-year institutions, whose athletic competition is governed by either the NCAA or the National Association of Intercollegiate Athletics (NAIA), and two-year institutions governed by the National Junior College Athletic Association (NJCAA).

The NCAA is divided into several divisions. Division I schools are the powerhouses of college sports. Therefore, Division I is the first choice of most of the best athletes, although many professionals do come from Division II or from the smaller colleges of the NAIA.

Each of those organizations—NCAA, NJCAA, and NAIA—allows its colleges a limited number of scholarships for each sport. Division I colleges have certain "head-count" sports. That means that every athlete in that sport who receives any amount of aid is counted as a scholarship recipient. In other words, any partial scholarship counts fully toward the total allowed for that sport. For the 1994–95 year, these are the maximum number of scholarships allowed in the "head-count" sports:

|            | *Men* | *Women* |
|------------|-------|---------|
| Basketball | 13    | 15      |
| Football   | 85    | —       |
| Gymnastics | —     | 10      |
| Ice hockey | 30    | —       |
| Tennis     | —     | 8       |
| Volleyball | —     | 12      |

All Division I sports other than the "head-count" sports and all Division II sports are called "equivalency" sports. The college is allowed a certain number of scholarships, but they can be split into any number of partial scholarships as long as they do not add up to more than the following limits:

|  | Men | Women |
|---|---|---|
| Archery | — | 5 |
| Badminton | — | 8 |
| Baseball | 11.7 | — |
| Bowling | — | 5 |
| Crew | — | 20 |
| Fencing | 4.5 | 5 |
| Field hockey | — | 11 |
| Golf | 4.5 | 6 |
| Gymnastics | 6.3 | — |
| Ice hockey | 18 | 18 |
| Lacrosse | 14 | 11 |
| Rifle | 4 | — |
| Skiing | 6.3 | 7 |
| Soccer | 9.9 | 11 |
| Softball | — | 11 |
| Squash | — | 9 |
| Swimming | 9.9 | 14 |
| Synchronized swimming | — | 5 |
| Team handball | — | 12 |
| Tennis | 9.9 | — |
| Track & cross-country | 14 | 16 |
| Volleyball | 4.5 | — |
| Water polo | 4.5 | 8 |
| Wrestling | 9.9 | — |

Division II institutions are permitted almost as many scholarships, with a total limit of sixty. This total does not include thirty-six football scholarships or ten basketball scholarships. Division III schools do not offer athletic scholarships.

It is important to know the rules involved in a scholarship. These include rules concerning eligibility, recruiting, and financial aid.

**Eligibility.** You can further or hinder your college career in several ways. Your first eligibility hurdle is academic. A new and controversial rule, adopted by the NCAA in 1989, denies scholarships to any high school athlete who fails to meet certain academic standards.

To enter a Division I school after August 1, 1995, and be eligible as a freshman you must graduate with a C average in at least thirteen full academic "core" courses. This includes three years of English and two years each of mathematics and social science. If your grade point average (GPA) is 2.5 or better (halfway between B and C), you need to score a total of at least 700 on the SAT or 17 on the ACT. If you barely squeak by with a 2.0 GPA, you need an SAT of 900 or an ACT of 21.

To be eligible for a Division II college, you need a 2.0 GPA and a total score of at least 700 on the SAT or 17 on the ACT.

Likewise, Division III institutions have their own regulations. To transfer from a two-year college, you must graduate or have acceptable grades.

If you want to compete as a college freshman you must register and be certified by the NCAA Initial-Eligibility Clearinghouse. Your counselors can obtain the red brochure and the student-release form by phoning (319) 337-1492.

Another eligibility hurdle to participating in college sports is amateurism. In the NCAA, you are allowed to be a professional in one sport and retain your amateur standing in another, but you must be an amateur in your scholarship sport. This means that you cannot sign a contract, secretly or otherwise, in that sport. It also means that you are ineligible if you sign a contract with an agent who will represent you later. Some agents have been known to risk their athlete's whole career by offering a secret contract. You will also be declared ineligible if you appear in commercials or give endorsements for products. You cannot allow your name to go into the professional draft.

**Recruiting.** The rules for college sports recruiting are rigid and severe. Be aware of any recruiters who make promises that seem too good to be true. You cannot be expected to be up-to-date on all the rules, especially since they change from time to time, but you can learn some. And whenever a recruiter offers you something or takes you for a visit, ask in advance if it violates any rule.

The most common recruiting rules have to do with "contacts." If a recruiter visits your home or school, that is a contact. A recruiter may not contact you more than three times at home and three times at school. Alumni are not allowed to contact you anywhere except on the college campus. You are allowed five all-expense-paid visits to colleges, but each visit must be no longer than forty-eight hours.

You must not accept contacts with anyone except officials. The NCAA guide states: "In addition to general recruiting regulations, no alumni, boosters, or representatives of a college's athletics interests can be involved in your recruiting. There can be no phone calls or letters from boosters."

Later, when you decide which scholarship to accept, you will sign a letter of intent. This letter is like a contract between you and the college, signaling the end of recruiting. After you have signed, no other college is allowed to recruit you. If you change your mind and go to another college, you will lose eligibility. But once you have signed, there is no longer any limit to the number of contacts you may receive.

**Financial aid.** The third set of rules applies to your scholarship. The financial aid you receive is limited to tuition, room and board, fees, and books. You are permitted no employment except during vacations. You will be given complimentary tickets to games, but these are for your friends and relatives. If you sell them, you risk losing your eligibility.

Everybody has read news stories about college super-athletes being given gifts, some as expensive as a house or car. Probably many thousands of athletes have sold complimentary tickets, called comps. Alumni have been known to give money to athletes. Favors are extended, from introducing male athletes to women to finding a job for the athlete's father. All are against the rules, and the NCAA enforces these rules.

The penalties to a college or university that breaks the rules are very harsh. Oklahoma University was placed on probation for three years in 1989 when an alumnus broke the rules and gave money to football players. The team was not allowed to play in bowl games for two years nor to receive money from television contracts in 1989. They could recruit only eighteen football players per year instead of twenty-five.

They estimate that they lost close to a million dollars each of those three years. You can harm your college by breaking the rules.

Your own penalties can be severe as well. You can be declared ineligible ever to play for that college. You may lose your scholarship and your degree. The college may be placed on probation, making it impossible for you to play in postseason playoff games.

In spite of these punishments, rules are broken for many reasons, but mainly for money and pride. Millions of dollars are involved in college football. A winning team can mean hundreds of thousands of dollars to its college. Winning or losing often means the coach keeps or loses his job. Wherever big money is involved, some people are bound to cheat, and unfortunately college sports are no exception. In addition to money, pride in the team causes some people, especially alumni, to break the rules.

To protect your good name, your honor, your school, and your future, you must know the rules and obey them.

## THE RECRUITING PROCESS

In addition to the rules, you should have some idea of how the recruiting process is carried out and how it will affect you.

First, a college must become interested in you as a prospective student and athlete. If you are all-state or state champion, you will have no problem. They probably know you, and many of them will try to recruit you if you have other qualities as well. But what if you are like most other high school athletes—good but not great? Most of the colleges in your area will know about you, but you may be after a larger school. How do you gain its attention?

You have to be realistic about how high you aim. Do you and your coach honestly believe you can make any college team in the country? Or are your hopes no better than Division III? If you did not make your league all-star team, the chances of your getting a football scholarship at Notre Dame or USC are not very high.

Look for several colleges on a level where you should be able to play. Whether you have fifty recruiters beating a path to your door or none at all, you should consider a lot more than a college's won-lost record. Keep in mind that you will likely spend at least four years in the college that you choose, where you might make lifetime friends and decisions that will affect the rest of your life. Don't make the choice lightly.

Of course, you want the best athletic program you can find. Usually the Division I schools have the top programs, the best coaches and facilities, and the best competition, but that is not always the case. Some smaller colleges may have coaches you would rather work with and learn from.

You will probably be better off in a college where athletes are given some sort of study supervision. You need a "brain coach" as well as a baseball coach. As you consider your options, find out the following information about each college: What percentage of freshmen graduate? What percentage of athletes are in your sport? Does the college continue to help athletes after their eligibility runs out? Consider the academic reputation of the college as well as its athletic reputation. Does it have the courses you want for your major? What is the student/professor ratio?

Consider other aspects of college life. Do you like the players and students? Are your favorite recreations available? What are your chances for a summer job? Does the college offer help in finding a job? How far away from home is the college, and do your parents like it or dislike it?

After you have looked into several colleges, you will be able to narrow your choices to the colleges where you want to be considered for a scholarship. Your next step is to attract their attention and interest. You, or somebody else, must put on a public relations campaign in your behalf.

Your best and easiest method is probably through your coaches. Sometime in your junior year of high school you should let them know you would like to earn a scholarship. If a coach likes you and thinks you are good enough, he or she can be of great help. Coaches have contacts at some colleges and can tip them off to watch you perform. Coaches can give you advice and even suggest a college that will suit your abilities.

Some high school athletes contact colleges of their choice by mail or in person to let them know of their interest. Send them clips of a local newspaper in which you were featured. Another possibility is actually to show them your best play. Many high schools film their games; you can copy some of your best moves. If the school does no filming, you might see if you can obtain a camcorder and let your parents film your games.

Once you are known to a college coach, that coach can decide if he or she is interested. If so, a recruiter will check your qualifications. If everything appears fine, a recruiter will be sent to interview you.

Before talking with you, the recruiter will check on your grades and any information about your general reputation in your school. If all is well, the recruiter will visit your coach and collect information about your natural ability, your training efforts, and your strengths and weaknesses as a player and as a person.

## THE INTERVIEW OR CAMPUS VISIT

When the recruiter is ready to talk to you, make sure you are well prepared. This will be like a job interview. You want to behave well to make a good impression. Don't turn off the recruiter with bad manners, bragging, shyness, being crude, or any other suspect behavior. If you are in doubt, ask your coach for some advice on how to act. Plan to take notes during the interview so you will remember each recruiter and whatever promises each one makes.

Have all your records available at the interview so you can answer all questions. Your athletic notebook or training diary can help you remember such things as how much weight you gained in the last year, your marks in the 40-yard dash, or the height of your vertical leap.

During this interview you may collect information about the college or its athletic program. You can ask such questions as: Do you have a weight training coach? What is the policy about conflicts between training or games and classes or lab schedules? You can also evaluate the honesty and character of the recruiter.

If the recruiter is impressed with you, he or she may want to visit your home. A good family relationship may help assure the recruiter of your personal stability. At this time, the recruiter may make you an offer. Take careful notes of exactly what you are offered. Don't accept the statement "full ride" without asking exactly what it covers. An official scholarship statement does not come until after you make your decision to accept an offer and sign the letter of intent. Therefore, you want an exact statement before you make your decision.

In other cases, you may be offered a campus visit before you have to make your decision. This expenses-paid trip will give you a chance to see the entire campus including all the athletic facilities. You will probably meet the head coach and be able to consider his or her style. You can talk with other players and students. They may take you to a game or a party. The more they do for you, the more interested they are in you. In that case, other colleges will probably be interested too. Try not to be carried away by any one college; keep your judgment sharp so that you can compare this college with all the other colleges you are considering.

Prepare yourself to be able to handle any recruiting pressure. If, instead of having to sell yourself to them, they are trying to sell themselves to you, then you know you have a choice. Ask how long you have to make up your mind. If two or more colleges are competing to recruit you, letting them know that will strengthen your position.

If, on the other hand, only one college is interested in you, don't delay. If you want to attend that college, be enthusiastic and let them know you are favorably impressed. Most colleges recruit more athletes than they can sign. If you delay, they may come up with your replacement before you decide.

If you are not offered a scholarship immediately, keep trying. Bill Serra of College Athletic Placement

Service in Asbury Park, New Jersey, says, "The athletic-scholarship world is like an iceberg. Only the tip is showing." He claims a 90 percent success rate in finding "rides" for about 500 men and women each year, but he charges a retainer fee of $400, plus $1,000 for a placement. Serra says, "Every year, grants go begging for lack of candidates."

If you fail to win a scholarship, it is not the end of your athletic career. There are other forms of financial aid. At some colleges and universities more than 75 percent of the students qualify for financial aid, and almost all are accepted on the basis of need. Once you are in college, almost all teams will accept walk-ons. That means you can try out for the team without being on an athletic scholarship. You have a chance to prove yourself.

## SUCCEED IN COLLEGE

Too many athletes go to college only to pursue one goal: to become professional athletes. Everything else, including schoolwork, takes a back seat. They waste a great opportunity, because college offers many possibilities. College can train you for whatever career you may choose outside of professional athletics. More generally, it can broaden your understanding of the world.

To be given a scholarship for a college education is like being given $40,000 to $80,000. To waste it is foolish. Only a little over one-third of NFL players have graduated from college. This means that after their short NFL career they either have to return to college or make a living without a college degree. Make graduation one of your main goals.

If your sport requires so much time that you cannot keep up with a full classload, then make up the necessary classes in summer school. Take a full load of the more difficult courses during your off-season.

Another main goal is success in your sport. In addition to your training and competition, there are important considerations that can help or hurt you.

Learn the system and the people. This means learning all the rules and obeying them. Avoid ticket-scalping, even if your teammates are doing it. Stay away from agents, even those who promise that nobody will ever know if you sign an illegal contract. Do not accept illegal gifts that might cause you to lose your eligibility. Consider changing your position. If you are only third string at quarterback and you believe you can play first string as a wide receiver, don't let pride stand in your way.

Reduce your chance of injury. Don't risk injury by playing while you are in poor condition. Stay in good condition all year. Eat well, rest, and warm up before every practice and game. In addition, you are more liable to sustain injuries if you play carelessly, so do your best to stay focused during practice and games. And when you are injured, be wary of painkillers.

One horror story about painkillers is told by the great basketball center Bill Walton: "At halftime, Dr. Cook said if I just took this shot of Xylocaine in my leg, it would be all right to go back out and play. I took the shot, felt good for about thirty-five seconds, limped through the rest of the game, and spent the next six weeks in a cast on crutches."

Don't let anyone, including your coach, run you off. Sometimes a coach and a player may not get along. Maybe he or she thinks you are not good enough, even though you are still only a first-year student. Your coach may want to turn your scholarship over to another player. He or she may try to make you quit by various methods, including ridiculing or benching you. Stay confident in yourself and your abilities. Try harder and get other players to support you and take your side.

Getting along in college means concentrating on being a good student and a good person. Work at it the way you work at your sport.

## MONITOR YOUR PROGRESS

It is a good idea to keep a journal of all your plays. When you make any play in your sport, keep track of it. You may think you will remember it, but chances are you will not. If you make a good play, write it down and study it so you will be able to do it again. If you make a bad move, write it down and see what you did wrong so you can do it right the next time. For example, in a round of golf you will swing many different clubs many times. If you keep a record of each stroke you miss and why it went wrong, you can check it over later to learn which shots you need to practice the most. A year later, you will be able to compare yourself now and then and know how much progress you are making.

If you practice shooting free throws every day, you will be able to tell the percentage of improvement a year later if you have kept a log. If you are a runner, a log of your workouts will help you decide why you were particularly strong or weak in various races.

Therefore, keep an athletic diary. Have an entry for each day. Even if you do nothing on a particular day, make a note of why you were idle. Enter the time of your workout, weather conditions, and personal conditions such as your weight, pulse rate, hours of sleep, and any illness or injuries. Record your workouts or game performances, and write down subjective thoughts about your progress. You can add notes about anything that might help you. Enter anything to aid your memory concerning your progress.

Another way to monitor your progress is to write down each of your goals, whether short-term or long-term. Then write down how close you came to reaching your goals. This not only acts as a checklist to remind you of your target, but it also keeps a record of your successes.

Also keep a list of roadblocks to progress. What caused you to fall short in your last game? Was it lack of skills or knowledge, bad decisions, poor conditioning, injuries, or worry about a relationship?

Use your notebook diary as a sort of third eye, where you can stand off and look at yourself objectively, as if you were your own coach.

## DECISION

Toward the end of your college career, you will need to make a decision. Will you attempt to become a pro? It may be an easy decision because it may be obvious that you are not good enough. If that is the case you will already know it, and the decision will be made. On the other hand, if you are obviously good enough, your decision will also be easy unless you are weighing another career against pro sports. Somewhere in the middle you may decide you have some chance of gaining a professional contract. Then it is up to you. The only danger is that you may believe you are better than you are. If you decide to try, it means hard work and the chance of failure. It may mean temporarily suspending your pursuit of another career and even putting off marriage. Still, you have much to gain and your small losses should be only temporary.

If you happen to be a great athlete, you might decide to enter the pro draft before you have used all of your collegiate eligibility. This is not an easy decision because it means giving up your college degree for the time being. But it is made easier by one possibility: you can return to college, according to certain stipulations, if you change your mind. If, for example, you enter the NBA draft after your junior year and you are disappointed in the interest the drafting teams show in you, you can return to college for your senior year. The decision to return to college and college athletics must be made within thirty days of the draft. You can do it only if you have no agent and have not accepted any money.

# Your Pro Contract: How to Get It

Professional sports teams pick the best athletes for their teams. If you are at the top of your sport, and you are skilled enough to qualify for or win the top tournaments, it is highly likely that you will be drafted. All you need is a good agent and knowledge of the rules.

But if you are borderline, like most excellent college athletes, you will need to develop your skills and prove yourself. You need to set goals and know where you want to go and how to get there.

In every sport, you must work your way up to become one of the best amateurs. In most sports, you must showcase your abilities to attract a pro contract. Your best opportunity to show off your abilities is in your school competition, but sometimes that is not enough. If you attend a small high school or an obscure college, your achievements may go unnoticed. Since sports differ from each other, you should examine your sport carefully to learn the best way to display your ability.

All the team sports conduct a draft. The pro teams get together at least once a year and make their choices from among all the available unsigned, usually college, players. The draft is how most players get a professional contract, but it is not the only way. Most sports offer other opportunities. If you want to break into pro sports, the following are a few things you should know about your particular sport.

**Baseball:** In total, baseball pays its athletes the highest salaries. The minimum salary increases every year with the cost of living. For 1997, the minimum salary was $150,000, but the average salary was $1,383,578. In 1976 the average salary was only $52,000. In 1995 the total paid out to players was over $923 million

The following is a list of the highest-paid baseball athletes for 1998:

| | |
|---|---|
| Barry Bonds, San Francisco | $11.4 million |
| Gary Sheffield, Florida | $10 million |
| Albert Belle, Chicago White Sox | $10 million |
| Greg Maddux, Atlanta | $ 9.6 million |
| Frank Thomas, Chicago White Sox | $ 9.3 million |
| Roger Clemens, Toronto | $ 8.2 million |
| Sammy Sosa, Chicago White Sox | $ 8 million |
| Andres Galarraga, Atlanta | $ 8 million |
| Mike Piazza, Los Angeles | $ 8 million |
| Ken Griffey Jr., Seattle | $ 7.9 million |
| John Smoltz, Atlanta | $ 7.7 million |
| Kenny Lofton, Cleveland | $ 7.5 million |
| Alex Fernandez, Florida | $ 7 million |
| Tom Glavine, Atlanta | $ 7 million |

The spring of 1991 saw a feeding frenzy of salary increases. These increases eventually led the team owners to attempt to stop it in 1994. The players' union rebelled against this. Unable to come to an agreement, the 1994 baseball season ended without a World Series. Many fans were outraged and felt cheated by what many thought of as greed by both the players and the owners. Although attendance was down when baseball resumed, everything has since returned to normal. However, many will remember the 1994 strike as something that devalued baseball.

Baseball pays excellent fringe benefits in the form of insurance, disability income, and pensions. And players are paid large amounts of money for endorsing various products. One agent claims that an MVP or Cy Young Award winner will collect up to a million dollars in added commercial benefits. With new TV contracts, baseball will receive half its income from television.

Baseball requires a variety of skills. You do not have to be especially tall or heavy, and it is possible to be a pro without being exceptionally talented in any one area as long as you are talented overall. You can be a pitcher if you can throw hard and with accuracy; you need not be a good hitter or fielder. If you are exceptionally quick, agile (with hands that can fasten onto a fast, hopping baseball), and have a good throwing arm, your defense can give you a chance of making it without being a talented hitter. If you have the natural hand-eye coordination necessary to hit a fast, curving baseball, you can probably fit in somewhere, even as a designated hitter. It helps if you can run fast, throw hard and straight, and field well, but a natural hitter is the most sought-after and highest-paid player in professional baseball.

How much a professional baseball player is paid sometimes depends on what team he plays for. In 1997, the average salary for the New York Yankees was $2.2 million. The Houston Astros averaged less, with $1.2 million, while the Pittsburgh Pirates averaged only $300,000.

In addition to those huge salaries in the major leagues, baseball has eighteen minor leagues where most players play for a year or more before making the majors. Most of the minor-league teams are farm teams belonging to one of the twenty-eight major-league clubs. If you are signed to a contract, you will probably be assigned to one of these minor-league teams until you prove yourself a big-leaguer. Salaries of minor leaguers can be anywhere from $850 a month in Class A up to a major-league figure, since some big-leaguers are "sent down" while injured or working out problems. Usually, a player who was paid a huge bonus to sign will receive more than the minimum salary.

Some American baseball players go to Japan and play for their league. Although the pay is substantially less in Japan than it is in the United States, baseball players such as Ralf Bryant and Tom O'Malley enjoy playing baseball in Japan. This move of professional ball players from the United States to Japan has been happening for a number of years, but recently Major League Baseball has turned to Japan for new talent.

Hideki Irabu, an all-star pitcher from Japan and hyped to be the next Ryan Nolan, joined the New York Yankees. He signed a four-year, $12.8 million contract with the Yankees. Although Irabu didn't perform as well as expected and was eventually sent to the minors, he would not be the last Japanese player to play in the major leagues in the United States. The Los Angeles Dodgers signed Hideo Nomo for $2.8 million a year. Masato Yoshii recently joined the New York Mets. Major League Baseball avoids drafting players who are already on a team. Instead it looks for amateur players.

Baseball conducts two drafts each year, usually drafting two or three hundred players from high school players, from college players who have completed their eligibility, or from free agents. If you are drafted but not signed to a contract within six months, you become a free agent. All current players who are not drafted become free agents. If you are a free agent, you can try out with any team willing to give you a chance.

A high school draftee could choose college and thus gain experience plus a degree while training to become major-league material. Since baseball has the most extensive minor-league system of any sport, a good player has ample opportunity to prove his worth. In addition to organized baseball, there are many semi-professional teams open to anybody who can play well enough, including high school and college players and any other free agents. Major-league teams have scouts all over the country looking for talented players. Therefore, wherever you play, if you are good enough you will likely be "discovered," especially if someone tips off a scout. You might help your own cause by getting your coach or manager or a sports writer to contact a scout.

**Basketball:** Individual players in the NBA are paid more than individuals in any other sport. The combined salary of NBA players was about $1 billion last year. The average salary of an NBA player is $2.6 million. Thirty-five of the 400 players in the NBA make more than $5 million per season. Sixty-five percent of the players are millionaires. There are also a number of players with $100 million contracts, including Kevin Garnett's record-breaking six-year $121 million deal. Salaries for NBA players have ballooned astronomically in recent years, and it is the salary issue that has led to a lockout. The NBA and the players union have come to blows concerning a salary-cap exception known as the Larry Bird clause. This clause allows a team to disregard the salary cap for certain free agents and to pay these players a salary above the cap. The league wants to eliminate or modify this clause, the players refuse, and the result was a lockout that seriously threatened the 1998–1999 basketball season.

Basketball requires quickness, agility, and remarkable accuracy in shooting. You also need a quickness of mind to see opportunities in a split second plus the ability to cooperate with other players for the betterment of the team. If you possess all these skills and are exceptionally tall, give basketball a chance. A few players under six feet have been successful, but they must be near the best in the world at shooting, passing, and dribbling. With the three-point line, a great outside shooter has a better chance. A few slow or relatively awkward players have been successful, but they were usually seven feet tall. You should also have endurance and be strongly built because the no-contact rules of basketball have been roughly shoved aside. The good pros have spent thousands of hours in practice. Unless you possess some or all the above skills, chances are you probably will not make it into the pros.

Basketball teams draft more than 200 players in June or July of each year. College players must complete their college eligibility before being drafted unless they ask to be drafted. Only about fifty new players make the rosters each year, leaving out hundreds of good players. Since some players continue to play and improve after college, it is possible that some of the players may eventually become good enough for the NBA.

If you are one of these players, what chance do you have? The Continental Basketball Association, the official developmental league of the NBA, employed 160 players on sixteen teams in 1994. Those players are paid $13,000 to $25,000 plus housing for five months of work. In addition, many Americans play pro basketball in Italy. There are summer basketball camps where some excellent players compete. Or, as a long shot, you might try to make the Olympic basketball team. But your best hope for the NBA is to improve over the summer and try out as a free agent for the next year.

Women's basketball has come a long way since the Women's Professional Basketball League folded in 1981. In addition to the women's American Basketball Association (ABL) that started in 1985, the NBA has created a women's division called the Women's National Basketball Association (WNBA). The WNBA was a triumphant success in its first year, more than doubling attendance projections and gaining high television ratings. The pay for both the ABL and the WNBA is, however, substantially lower than that of the NBA. The ABL pays its players an average of $80,000 while the WNBA pays an average of $35,000.

**Football:** The average salary of a player in the National Football League is $795,000 a year. Deion Sanders's six-year $30 million deal plus a $12 million signing bonus with the Dallas Cowboys has made him the highest-paid defensive player in NFL history. Troy Aikman, also of the Dallas Cowboys, receives about $6 million a year. A few other players—Dan Marino (Miami), John Elway (Denver), and Steve Young (San Francisco)—receive about $5 million a year.

Gene Upshaw, president of the NFL Players Association, explained why football players are paid less. "Free agency doesn't work. The owners aren't going to bid for players. Why should [an owner] go out to increase his payroll? He's not going to make any more money." The reason is because each NFL team receives a certain amount of money from its share of television income. This amount remains the same even if the quality of players drops off. Upshaw also complains that the average football career is too short—just over three years.

Football requires a variety of qualities. All players should be rugged, physically and mentally, to survive strenuous contact, and they must be able to put the success of the team ahead of all other goals. Coaches look for speed and quickness at all positions, and height and weight are expected to be greater than for players in most other sports. Linemen need exceptional strength, both natural and acquired. Running backs, wide receivers, and defensive backs need great speed coupled with unusual agility to change direction. Linebackers rely on the lineman's strength and the defensive back's speed. A quarterback needs a good throwing arm and exceptional accuracy plus the split vision of basketball players, a quickness in scrambling away from tacklers, and greater presence of mind than any other athlete. Other special qualities may win you a pro contract as a punter or a place kicker.

After the winter bowl games, the NFL teams draft 336 players in twelve rounds. The top draft choices receive large sums of money for signing, but only half of the draftees ever make a team. A few wait to be activated if one of the regular players is injured, but the others, along with about 1,200 good players who were not drafted, become free agents. They may try out for any team. The training camps in late summer include many free agents. A few are actually signed to contracts. Most, however, cannot make an NFL team, and, unlike in some other sports, there are no minor leagues where players can improve their skills. Some free agents play in the Canadian league, where a good player can earn more than $100,000 a year. But linebacker Reggie Williams said, "Going to the Canadian Football League is identity suicide." If you do not play in the NFL or CFL, you can only keep in shape, perhaps by playing on a semipro team, and try again later. Occasionally, when a team loses a player to injuries, they sign a free agent in mid-season.

**Hockey:** The National Hockey League (NHL) has a provision under the new collective bargaining agreement that allows young players a limited form of free agency. This rule, in effect, allows rich teams to lure players from not-so-rich teams with huge signing bonuses. Joe Sakic, Colorado, is the biggest money-maker of the 1997–1998 season with a salary of $17 million, which includes a $15 million signing bonus. Chris Gratton, Philadelphia, comes in second with a $10 million salary and a signing of $9 million. Eric Lindros, Philadelphia, has a salary of $7.5 million.

There are several minor leagues where players may earn a living for their six-month season while they prepare for the NHL. Hockey is played in Europe, particularly in Austria, Switzerland, and Germany. Some United States players earn good salaries abroad, although the teams limit the number of foreign players.

The American Hockey League (AHL), with seventeen teams in the eastern United States and Canada, furnishes almost two-thirds of the National Hockey League players. Pay for most players not on an NHL contract runs from about $25,000 to a few near $60,000. The International Hockey League (IHL), with seventeen teams stretched from Atlanta to San Diego, pays their more experienced players as much as $60,000 to $80,000 a year and promotes fewer to the NHL. In recent years, three lesser leagues made up of thirty-two teams have added a starting place for young professionals.

A hockey player must be even more of a team player than a basketball player. Instead of running speed, a hockey player needs skating ability. He must also spend thousands of hours learning to handle the puck with his hockey stick while skating fast. Other than those differences, he needs the same quickness, agility, endurance, and accuracy as a basketball player, but height is not as important. A goalie can forgo some of those talents, but he must be exceptionally quick and rugged. Today's hockey players concentrate more on offense and less on defense; therefore, you can help your cause by learning to be a good defensive player.

Young hockey prospects must first learn to skate well. At the age of nine they can begin playing age-group hockey in the youngest of the four age-groups, nine-ten. The determining factor in learning hockey is finding playing time. This can be very hard depending on where you live. Only in Canada and a small part of the United States are winters cold enough to freeze ponds or outdoor rinks, allowing hockey to be played all winter. (Although two hockey players have come from San Diego, ice rinks are rare enough in most areas to all but prohibit hockey.) A young player can develop well by playing the equivalent of thirty to forty games a year.

Only a few high schools in the United States provide this opportunity.

Tom Barrasso did it the Canadian way and found a way to play about 100 games a year. He went directly to the Minnesota North Stars from high school in Massachusetts and won a first-team NHL all-star berth in his first season. A few other U.S. hockey players have made the NHL immediately out of high school, but it is rare, and many experts believe it is wiser to play more before signing. For instance, the Pro Elite Draft Development League in Hingham, Massachusetts, prepares young players for the NHL with a ten-week summer season, during which they play against minor pros and a few NHL players.

The NHL's July draft is similar to those in other team sports, but the rules are a little different. If you are drafted out of high school but want to go on to college, your team retains draft rights to you until six months after your college career ends. While you can play minor league hockey instead of going to college, it is a better idea to take those four years to earn a degree and improve your game.

Good Canadian hockey players usually go into Canadian Junior A leagues. These leagues are like minor leagues, with overnight trips to play in other cities. The players are paid only the cost of their expenses, even though they live like minor professionals. Their goal is to make the NHL, and many do. American hockey players make up to five to eight percent of the league. However, Syd DeRoner, former age-group coach, says, "An American boy loses nothing if he goes to a good hockey school in the United States." This is because American college hockey has improved greatly in the past twenty years.

Your chances may depend on the climate in which you live. Once you learn the game, you have ample opportunity to prove your worth in college or the minor leagues.

**Soccer:** Soccer is the most popular sport in the world, with a following of billions of people, yet it has never been popular in the United States. The North American Soccer League failed, as did the Major Indoor Soccer League. The huge difference in soccer popularity in the United States and in other countries around the world is evidenced in the salaries paid. The top salary for the current players in Major League Soccer in the United States is $236,750.

The following is a list of the top three moneymakers in soccer in the world:

| | |
|---|---|
| Ronaldo, Brazil | $34.1 million |
| Denilson, Brazil | $31.2 million |
| Rivaldo, Brazil | $29.6 million |

But according to the United States Soccer Federation, all this is about to change. In the next twelve years, more than $50 million will be spent to develop soccer. Project 40 is a program that transfers college soccer players to professional teams in exchange for room, board, and scholarships. The federation wants to train more players at an early age. Three hundred sixty players from ages thirteen to twenty-one will be training with national team coaches at least seventy-five days a year. The goal is for the United States to win the World Cup in the year 2010. "This is no little plan. This is a vision on a grand scale," said U.S. Soccer Federation president Alan Rothenberg.

Success at soccer requires running speed, high endurance, and exceptional skill in directing the ball with both feet and head. Team cooperation is absolutely essential, and it helps to have a little of the football quarterback's presence of mind because the situation changes rapidly whenever you have the ball. A goalie must be quick and agile and rugged in diving for the ball. Height is not important. You will run off any excess weight.

If you are a superstar by American standards, you are allowed to play for an international team, but the competition is fierce. The first American to break into the highest level of international pro soccer was two-time UCLA All-American Paul Caligari, who signed in West Germany in 1987. The U.S. World Cup team in 1994 included John Harkes, Ernie Stewart, Thomas Dooley, Roy Wegerle, Tab Ramos, Eric Wynalda, and Brad Friedel, all under contract to European pro teams. After the United States' strong showing against Brazil in 1994, five other members of the team received offers from Europe.

A semiprofessional league, called the American Indoor Soccer Association, pays its players about $2,500 a month for the five-month season. The U.S. Interregional Soccer League (USISL), organized in 1994 as a Division III Professional league, pays players $60 to $300 per game, with a few receiving as much as $1,200 a month. Each of the seventy-one teams has twenty-six players, with eighteen active on game day. The National Professional Soccer League began its thirteenth season in October 1996. This indoor league has twelve teams, with sixteen players per team. They play forty games plus playoffs in April. Players are under contract, and their salaries are confidential.

The largest and oldest pro soccer league is the English Football League with ninety-two teams.

With so many successful foreign teams and with thousands of high school teams in the United States, MLS hopes to be more successful than its predecessors.

**Golf:** Golf's recent rise in popularity, especially among younger kids, can be traced back to a twenty-one-year-old kid named Eldrick (Tiger) Woods. He won the first tournament he entered as well as the first major tournament: The Masters. He won with a record-breaking 18-under-par 270, one shot less than a thirty-two-year record set by Jack Nicklaus. Woods helped bring golf to a younger generation and made the sport hot. In one poll, Woods scored the second highest in popularity behind Colin Powell.

Tiger Woods led the pack as the top PGA (Professional Golfers Association) money winner of 1997. He earned almost $500,000 from the Masters alone. Woods won almost $2 million while the top ten men each won over $1 million. In the European PGA, Colin Montgomerie earned the most with $613,948. Anniko Sorenstam led the Ladies Professional Golfers Association (LPGA) with a little more than $1 million. The Senior PGA for golfers over 50, often offers top money to winners. Prize money is often more for the Senior PGA than for the regular PGA. Hale Irwin led the Senior PGA with more than $2 million. The top seven golfers in the Senior PGA each won more than $1 million. Let's look at the career earnings of some golfers:

| | |
|---|---|
| Greg Norman | $11,812,918 |
| Tom Kite | $10,286,177 |
| Fred Couples | $ 8,838,087 |

| | |
|---|---|
| Nick Price | $ 8,728,774 |
| Mark O'Meara | $ 8,426,774 |
| Payne Stewart | $ 8,426,259 |
| Tom Watson | $ 8,307,277 |
| Davis Love III | $ 8,183,552 |
| Corey Pavin | $ 8,130,356 |
| Scott Hoch | $ 7,781,017 |

In 1994, the prize money for tournaments amounted to more than $19 million. American Brian Watts, little known in the United States, won more than $1.2 million on the 1994 Japanese PGA tour, where Jumbo Osaki of Japan won $4,154,680.

A good golfer can be old or young, tall or short, overweight or thin, and relatively unathletic. To be great in golf you must be exceptionally accurate. Quickness helps, enabling you to swing faster and thus hit longer shots. Other than quickness and accuracy, you need great mental discipline, which allows you to practice by the hour and avoid errors during competition. You also need maturity and self-control to stand the constant travel and competition on ever-changing golf courses. Gary McCord, pro golfer and TV commentator, says, "The tour can beat you up." Tommy Aaron said, "Golf is mostly a game of failures." And Gary Player said, "When you play for fun, it's fun. But when you play golf for a living, it's a game of sorrows. You're never happy."

To have a chance to play in professional tournaments, you must qualify. To play in the U.S. Open, you must compete in qualifying tournaments. To play on the PGA tour, you must qualify in a series of tournaments that culminate with the Qualifying School's pressure-packed 108-hole tournament. The top forty golfers join the top 130 money winners and a few exempted former champions on the PGA tour for the next year. You must also satisfy other PGA requirements, including experience and financial stability.

If you are not good enough to play on the PGA tour, you still have many options. There are various amateur levels on which you can play to improve your game. There are three amateur levels: U.S. Amateur, U.S. Junior Amateur, and the Mid-Amateur Championship. There are also the British Amateur and the Amateur Public Links competitions.

Unlike other professional sports, in which an athlete can compete for only a few years before retiring, golfers can play professional all their lives. The PGA Tour is open to those under fifty, while the Senior PGA is open to those over fifty. Another bonus is that the prize money on the Senior PGA Tour is often higher than on the PGA tour. Here are the leading money winners for the 1997 Senior PGA Tour:

| | |
|---|---|
| Hale Irwin | $2,003,864 |
| Gil Morgan | $1,665,762 |
| Isao Aoki | $1,203,728 |
| Jay Sigel | $1,173,581 |
| David Graham | $1,123,558 |
| John Bland | $1,108,397 |
| Graham Marsh | $1,047,976 |
| Larry Gilbert | $ 902,816 |
| Dave Stockton | $ 805,016 |
| Hugh Baiocchi | $ 770,468 |

Golf also offers women an opportunity to earn more

money than in most other sports. Here is a list of the top money winners in the 1997 LPGA Tour:

| | |
|---|---|
| Anniko Sorenstam | $1,055,039 |
| Karrie Webb | $ 929,981 |
| Kelly Robbins | $ 803,674 |
| Chris Johnson | $ 630,879 |
| Tammie Green | $ 580,813 |

**Tennis:** The growing popularity of tennis may be the result of television cameras that can cover the entire court. Tennis has become a gold mine for professionals, both men and women. Men's professional tennis alone collects around $400 million each year from prize money, television rights, endorsements, and other income. The down side of this is that the money goes to a small number of players. Unlike golf, for example, where dozens of players have a chance to win, tennis is dominated by a small number of players.

In the men's category, there is no doubt that Pete Sampras has dominated the sport. Some say he is possibly the greatest tennis player ever. He is also the top money winner for 1997.

Here is a list of the standings for 1997:

| | |
|---|---|
| Pete Sampras | $3,905,078 |
| Patrick Rafter | $2,432,084 |
| Gustavo Kuerten | $1,505,213 |
| Yevgeny Kafelnikov | $1,421,392 |
| Michael Chang | $1,327,720 |

Women's tennis was dominated by sixteen-year-old Martina Hingis, who became the youngest female to win a major event in the twentieth century. She also became the seventh woman ever to win three of the four Grand Slam titles.

Here is a list of the top women moneymakers for 1997:

| | |
|---|---|
| Martina Hingis | $3,126,036 |
| Iva Majoli | $1,139,537 |
| Lindsay Davenport | $1,133,106 |
| Jana Novotna | $ 966,215 |
| Monica Seles | $ 862,580 |

These players earn their huge sums by playing a grueling schedule for the entire year. Many of the top players are injured each year. Ivan Lendl said, "There is too much play, too much stress, and that is what is causing the injuries." The Association of Tennis Professionals managed to wrest control of the tournament schedule from the Men's International Professional Tennis Council in 1989.

Tennis requires quickness, agility, and considerable accuracy as well as some endurance and strength. With those qualifications and thousands of hours of practice, you can play well, but to win you must have a special kind of adaptiveness. Each shot requires you to move into position, sometimes in an instant. Faster than you have time to think, you must make a decision on how to hit the ball. Your shot selection is based upon the time required to reach a position, the position of your opponent, the percentage of success you are capable of for each potential shot, and the percentage of success your opponent will have if you hit that shot. Thus, you need a mind like a computer, programmed by training and by constant monitoring between points.

Breaking into this highly lucrative profession is fairly straightforward. You merely play in tournaments, working your way up through the age-group rankings and into school and college competition until you are good enough to win some matches in national tournaments. Your next step is the satellite circuit, something of a minor league, where you can win little money but can begin to win points toward your international ranking. One point will rank you at about 1,500th in the world. Winning a satellite circuit will gain twenty-five to thirty-five points, enough to rank you in the 300s. If you do well on the satellite circuit, you can move up to the challenger events, which award prize money of $25,000 to $75,000 plus about thirty points for winning one tournament. Only 128 players are good enough to compete at Wimbledon, sixteen of them from a qualifying tournament the week before.

The catch, in tennis, is that some young players lack opportunity. A budding tennis player needs a court, fairly expensive equipment, a good coach, and long hours of practice. As a result, many good athletes who lack these resources have been unable to reach their full potential in tennis. If you have access to tennis courts and your parents encourage you to take lessons, take advantage of the opportunity. If you focus your abilities and desire on the game, you should improve quickly. If, however, you can't find a regular place to play but love tennis and are skilled enough to beat most of your opponents, don't be discouraged. With a little effort, you can find a public recreation program to get you started. If you have talent, you'll be able to find someone to help you, but you must take the initiative. It is not as easy as joining a basketball shootout in a schoolyard.

**Boxing:** The largest winnings in sports go to the few boxers at the top. In 1988, Mike Tyson knocked out Michael Spinks in 1 minute, 31 seconds of the first round. Tyson's prize for that short fight amounted to more than $21 million, and Spinks received $13.5 million for losing. In 1996, Tyson earned $30 million for knocking out Frank Bruno.

In the sport of boxing, only those on the top can expect to earn the multimillion-dollar purses. Fighters such as Evander Holyfield can earn millions just to fight. Win or lose, they still make millions. In the now infamous Holyfield and Tyson fight, $35 million was to go to the winner and $30 to the loser. Despite the fact that Tyson was disqualified for biting Holyfield's ear, he still earned more than $20 million. He was fined $3 million and ordered to pay court fees.

While the big money may be enticing, boxing has a dark side. Many boxers do not earn enough to make a living, and many suffer serious injuries, including brain damage from the repeated pounding to the head. Former middleweight champion Rocky Graziano said, "Fighting is the only racket where you're almost guaranteed to end up as a bum." And the general atmosphere of boxing is somewhat less than glamorous. Ed "Too Tall" Jones, a great football lineman who tried boxing, said, "I have never been around so many crummy people in all my days."

A good boxer must be even better than a tennis player in adapting to a changing situation. He must be as rugged, mentally and physically, as a football linebacker. He should be as quick and agile as a basketball player, and he needs the endurance of a middle-distance runner. He needs the strength of a shot putter for a knockout punch. His size makes little difference because there are many different weight divisions.

Although it is difficult to work up to the multimillion-dollar payoffs, it is relatively easy to try. Your route is through the amateur ranks, working up through Golden Gloves tournaments and possibly the Olympic Games.

When you decide to turn pro, your main effort should be to obtain a capable and honest manager. Many boxers have lost most of their winnings to crooked handlers. Joe Louis, one of the greatest ever, lived in poverty. His handlers did not leave him enough money to pay his taxes.

**Bowling:** The Professional Bowlers Association of America (PBA) is the major league of bowling. The PGA has almost 4,000 members competing for millions of dollars on the annual tour. Walter Ray Williams Jr. became the first man to hit the $2 million mark in career earnings, with other competitors close behind.

Bowling is losing its popularity with the television audience. Low ratings and a decreasing number of big-money sponsors has led to the slow demise of bowling on television.

Here is a list of the top winners in the PBA for 1997:

| | |
|---|---|
| Parker Bohn III | $166,320 |
| W. R. William Jr. | $162,914 |
| Pete Weber | $158,184 |

*Ladies Profesional Bowlers Tournament*

| | |
|---|---|
| Wendy McPherson | $117,125 |
| Carol Gianotti-Black | $ 93,300 |
| Liz Johnson | $ 79,150 |

The Ladies Pro Bowlers Tour schedules almost as many tournaments as the men, and prizes are almost as high. With expenses estimated at $750 per tournament, you must place in the top twenty-four to break even, not counting your travel expenses. The LPBT also has regional tournaments in which you can experience professional competition on your way up.

Bowling is a game of accuracy, with only moderate strength and endurance needed. Training requires you to spend a lot of time in a bowling alley, practicing and honing your skills. Age is the least important criterion in bowling. Norm Duke won a tournament in 1983, before he was nineteen. Buzz Fazio won in 1965 when he was almost fifty-seven. In 1993, the best players were in their thirties.

Bowling is one of the easiest sports to break into. All you have to do is be good enough to roll a high average in one of the thousands of leagues. Your most difficult problems come at the beginning, when you're trying to find time and places to practice plus someone to train you. As an amateur bowler, you will join the American Bowling Congress. The ABC has about 5 million members. Your scores will be recorded and you will have an official average. To join the PBA and become eligible to compete in pro tournaments, a man must have an official average of 190 and a woman must average 175.

Competing in pro tournaments is costly, since you need expenses for travel and living. Only a few bowlers are good enough to make a living at it, although many more try. The Ladies Professional Bowlers Tour has about 200 competitors. Wendy Macpherson earned $117,125 on the 1997 LPBT.

**Horse Racing:** Money follows the racehorses to more than 100 tracks in the United States, and so the demand for jockeys is higher than for players in most other sports. There are about 2,200 qualified jockeys in the United States.

A top jockey might be paid $25,000 for a first-call contract, $10,000 for second call, and $5,000 for third call. If you are not called by a trainer who has you under contract, you are free to ride for any trainer. You will receive $25 to $50 per ride plus 10 percent of the purse for coming in first and 5 percent for second or third. (The winning horse gets 55 to 60 percent of the total purse, with 20 to 22 percent for second and 12 to 15 percent for third.)

In 1989, Willie Shoemaker retired as a jockey at the age of 57. However, he still holds the record for the greatest number of races won. Shoemaker won almost 9,000 races and more than $100 million in purses. Although Chris McCarron has won fewer than 7,000 races, his purse winnings total almost $200 million. Laffit Pincay Jr. comes behind McCarron with $194 million, having won 8,497 races over a period of thirty-one years. Julie Krone is the top female jockey. She has been the top money earner from 1986 to 1996, earning more than $5 million in 1996.

Size is one of the most important requirements for jockeys since horses carry a specified weight in a race. Shoemaker is 4'11" tall and weighs ninety-five pounds. Danny Winnick, at 5'2" and 100 pounds, decided to try to be a jockey when he finished high school even though he had never ridden a horse. He learned in three years. Women have a natural advantage in size, and they began competing with men in 1968. If your natural weight is around 100 pounds, you need only some strength, a lot of courage, good balance, and quick reflexes, and you must develop excellent judgment of pace and racing tactics. Most of your practice will come from actually riding in races, but it would certainly help to be an experienced rider before you try to race.

Jockey Patrick Day points out another qualification for a winning jockey: "A racehorse is a hypersensitive animal. He can sense if a jockey isn't feeling well, is upset or scared. The hands and reins the jockey uses on a horse are like a telephone people use to communicate. It's a very delicate situation between jockey and horse. A rider's attitude has a lot to do with the way a horse runs."

If you are small enough to be a jockey, you may earn a chance to ride by working around the stables. After you learn to care for horses, a trainer may let you begin as an exercise rider. After a year of "riding works" (daily morning rides), you can apply for an apprentice license if you are eighteen years old and have ridden two races under the eyes of the track stewards. An apprentice can be a licensed freelance apprentice or a contract apprentice. Under a contract, you are restricted to riding for one stable, but you will receive better overall training. A freelancer's certificate allows you to ride for any trainer. You must ride thirty-five winners before you receive your journeyman's license.

You must pass a written test to obtain a qualifying license. When a judge says you are ready, you receive a provisional license and you can ride in parimutuel races under probation. When you prove yourself, a judge awards you an "A" license with no restrictions.

**Harness Racing:** Harness drivers are paid 5 percent of their winnings, but the top drivers often negotiate for bonuses of a higher percentage. Mack Lobell, one of the greatest trotters ever to pull a sulky, won $523,150 in one race, a good payoff for the driver.

Here is a list of the top money earners in harness racing:

| | |
|---|---|
| Michael LaChance | $8,408,231 |
| John Campbell | $8,180,991 |
| Jack Moiseyev | $6,345,477 |
| Doug Brown | $5,539,627 |
| Tony Morgan | $5,201,715 |

While age, size, and sex are not criteria for drivers, fewer than one percent of the drivers are women. You must learn how to handle horses  proper pace, and tactics. If sprinting is 90 percent natural talent and 10 percent acquired skills, harness racing is probably just the opposite.

You must work your way up to become one of the drivers who make a good living. Most drivers began as stable boys and assistants to trainers, gradually working up to the opportunity to drive at the matinee meetings. There they can earn a license. Champion driver Bill Haughton says, "I do not know a prominent driver today who was not an expert with a rub rag long before he learned how to handle a whip."

You must be at least sixteen years old for a county fair license and eighteen for a raceway license. You do not have to be as light as a jockey. Drivers have won big races in their seventies, and there are some excellent women drivers.

**Auto Racing:** Most drivers are paid secret retainers rumored to be more than a million dollars. The purses in auto racing are often quite high. The purse for the Indy Brickyard was a NASCAR-record of $4.97 million. Jeff Gordon emerged as a top driver by winning both the Daytona 500 and the Winston Million bonus.

Many drivers are needed to drive in the Grand Prix, Indy-type, stock car, sport car, drag, and midget racing. Prize money runs into many millions, much of it from advertising money. The driver retains about 30 percent to 50 percent of his winnings.

Driving a race car requires quick reflexes, which improve with practice. It's a dangerous sport that requires courage because death is always a possibility. It requires great concentration. Bobby Allison said, "The margin of error is very, very narrow." It requires some strength and endurance to handle a car at such speeds for hours. And it requires good eyesight and keen judgment to grasp new situations at top speed.

Competition in race cars is more complicated than in most sports because of the many types of events and organizations that sponsor races. To begin to understand the setup, you need to know the meaning of USAC, CART, NASCAR, SCCA, IMSA, NARA and IHRA.

USAC, the United States Auto Club, sponsors the Indianapolis 500 as well as other Indy-type races. They also have a program in which you can work up with stock cars, midgets, and sprints. To become a member you must be twenty-one or older and qualify in experience.

CART, Championship Auto Racing Teams, has only a few hundred members, but it challenges USAC by sanctioning some Indy-type races.

NASCAR, the National Association for Stock Car Auto Racing, sponsors close to 2,000 races on almost 100 tracks for standard production-line cars.

SCCA, the Sports Car Club of America, sponsors amateur and professional racing in many types of road races. Thousands of members race in all the classes of races for a wide variety of cars.

IMSA, the International Motor Sports Association, has a small membership made up solely of active participants, but it sponsors the Camel GT series in competition with SCCA, and it also sponsors a series of races for low-cost cars.

NARA, the North American Rally Association, also challenges SCCA by sponsoring road rallies.

IHRA, the International Hot Rod Association, sponsors more than a dozen kinds of drag races.

Income for drivers is also complicated since drivers are paid in many ways. NASCAR credits drivers with their earnings, which are substantial. In 1994, Dale Earnhardt won $3,400,733 in Winston Cup driving, his third year over $3 million. Ten other drivers won more than $1 million. These winnings are split with the owners of the racing cars. Drivers are paid salaries by the owners, and most salaries are kept secret. Drivers and owners are also paid endorsements. In 1994, NASCAR held the first Brickyard 400 at Indianapolis, with $3.2 million in prize money.

Income varies depending on the individual and type of race. IMSA drivers are paid retainers of about $150,000 for a top driver and $45,000 for a rising star. Formula Atlantic drivers are not paid retainers; their income comes from personal sponsors and prize money. The Winston Drag Racing series awards $18 million in prizes for nineteen races.

A few drivers who own their own cars collect both ways, but car ownership is not always profitable. It costs $40,000 an hour to run a NASCAR stock car and an estimated $269,000 an hour to race a Formula One car. Only since large corporations have begun to put money into racing for advertising purposes has auto racing become so profitable.

Some beginners also own their own cars, which are much less expensive. For many would-be drivers, car ownership is the only opportunity they have to race. The most difficult part of working up to the big-money races is finding somebody who will let you drive a car. Trying to find a car to drive is like going in circles: You won't be given a car to drive until you have some experience, and you can't get the experience without a car to drive.

Another obstacle that beginners face is that the quality of the car is often more important than the ability of the driver. This means you cannot make a good showing with your driving skills alone. If you drive your own car, another important qualification would be your ability as a mechanic.

Try volunteering as part of the crew on a racing team. You may be allowed to take a racing car for a warmup, but more important, you will learn. There are a number of possibilities open to you: owning your car, volunteering on a crew, owning a minimum-level car if you can rake up a few thousand dollars, seeking opportunities to drive for someone, and studying at one of the more than seventy drivers' schools conducted by the Sports Car Club of America. Like all things, you can improve your skills by practicing. Although auto racing is a sport dominated mostly by men, there have been women drivers.

**Rodeo:** The Pro Rodeo Cowboys Association sanctions more than 750 rodeos each year, more than half in the United States and Canada. Total prize money for the sanctioned events amounts to more than $20 million.

A professional athlete is not paid to compete. Instead each person who wants to compete needs to spend his or her own money, usually amounting to thousands of dollars for traveling expenses and entry fees. The International Professional Rodeo Association sanctions more than 500 rodeos. Although individual earnings are rising, most participants are unable to make a living on their earnings alone. In order to win the top spot in their sport, each person needs to compete in 80 to 125 rodeos a year.

Dan Mortenson was the Champion All-Around Cowboy for 1997 and earned $184,559. His career earnings total almost $1 million.

Some young men seem to be natural riders, possessing the balance and agility needed to stay on a bucking bronco or a twisting bull. In addition, they need a tough mental attitude because injuries are frequent and often serious. For bulldogging and steer wrestling, they must be strong and quick-acting.

To become a rodeo competitor, you must first learn the skills. There are rodeo schools where you can train. You can enter local and regional competition. When you are good enough you can try the national circuit.

If you are good at bronco riding or the other events—bull riding, steer wrestling (bulldogging), calf roping, bareback riding, and team roping—your main obstacle will be injuries. Serious injuries are common, and they are the highest price you will have to pay for success. World champion saddle bronco rider Dan Mortensen suffered a disabling concussion and bit a hole through his lip when his head struck a horse's head. Trainer

Rich Blyn, who oversees treatment in the Mobile Sportsmedicine Center, says, "If you don't love this sport, you don't do it."

Women compete in barrel races around a triangular course. Barrel racing is a multimillion-dollar sport. Kristie Peterson was the 1997 barrel racing champion. Her earnings total $54,955. Her career earnings total $694,542. Almost 1,000 women belong to the Professional Women's Rodeo Association. About eighty women compete in bareback bronco riding, bull riding, and team and calf roping. About ten rodeos each year are for women only, but prize money is low. You must pay to obtain a permit to begin competing.

**Track and Field:** Although not officially a professional sport, track offers substantial monetary returns. There are those, such as Carl Lewis, Florence Joyner Griffith (who died in 1998), and Michael Johnson, who can make over a million dollars. While not many can make millions, many can still make a good living. The International Amateur Athletic Federation (IAAF) has said it expects to hand out approximately $19 million at seven major championships over the next two years. Many of these athletes also earn money through endorsement deals.

Track and field is experiencing a decrease in viewership and popularity. A $2 million, 150-meter match race between Michael Johnson and Donovan Bailey, called the "World's Fastest Human," was staged to attract fans. But it came up short when Johnson suffered an injury in the middle of the race.

Track and field requires various kinds of abilities. Sprinters need great natural speed; distance runners need natural endurance and the willingness to train hard.

Middle-distance runners need a combination of speed and endurance. Hurdlers must have speed plus agility. Jumpers need spring, throwers need arm strength, they all need agility. Pole vaulters need speed, strength, agility, and courage. They all need the will to train for years before they have a chance to reach the top.

More than most other sports, track requires you to work up through the amateur ranks. When you are good enough you will find the opportunities for earning appearance money, shoe contracts, endorsements, Grand Prix money, and prize money in road races.

## OTHER SPORTS

**Air Racing:** There are no full-time racing pilots, but almost all pilots have commercial jobs. Only a few races award prizes, and since the airplanes are expensive, pilots gain little profit.

**Archery:** Many professionals are teachers, with little opportunity to compete for money. The pros are fully sponsored by manufacturers who hope to profit from the advertising. Only a few women compete as pros.

**Billiards:** The Professional Billiards Association has seen an enormous growth in billiards competition, especially the women's competition. The billiards Class Tour offered a purse of $40,000. The purses for women's competition also grew by $700,000 among all WPBA professionals. Recently the women's purses and number of events surpassed their male counterparts. A top-ranking woman can easily earn $100,000 a year.

The WPBA ranks more than 200 players, but only about forty of these are touring professionals. Each tournament has about twelve qualifying spots, which are usually filled by local regional competition.

**Chess:** In 1997, for the first time in history, a computer defeated a grandmaster chess champion. IBM's computer known as Deep Blue beat world chess champion Garry Kasparov and raised several issues about artificial intelligence versus human intelligence.

Chess is a sport that offers very little monetary reward unless you're at the top of the ranks.

**Cutting:** The National Cutting Horse Association runs seven major cuttings a year, with 2,500 participants and $17 million in purses.

**Cycling:** According to Jack W. Simes of the U.S. Professional Cycling Federation, professional cycling is the second-largest sport, next to soccer. He says there are about 1,000 licensed professionals in the world. "They can earn anywhere from a thousand to one million dollars."

Most of the big cycling races are in Europe's Grand Prix events. Although it is not an extremely popular sport in the United States, a few Americans have been successful in these races. You must progress through the amateur ranks until you are good enough to become a professional. There are no women professionals.

The National Cycling League (NCL International) is made up of fifteen teams of eleven riders each, based in the United States, Europe, Canada, and Mexico. Races, on one-kilometer courses on the streets of major cities, are watched by local spectators and on television. These are team races, with points scored on every third lap, called "sprint laps." NCL riders earn salaries from $250 to $1,800 per race.

**Extreme Sports:** Extreme Sports, a term coined in the early '90s to describe alternative sports, has become very popular among men ages 18 to 35. Extreme sports focus on the high-risk, sometimes dangerous, aspects of athletics. Essentially, the thrill and the rush of adrenaline provide the purpose and incentive for these athletes to participate in extreme sports. Types of extreme sports include: snowboarding, sky-surfing, free-climbing, in-line skating, barefoot water-skiing, wakeboarding, street luge, snocross, and long-distance marathon running (whose distance can range from 30 to 300 miles). Many of these sports are variations of preexisting sports. For example, street luge evolved from the popular winter sport; wakeboarding is a combination of surfing, skateboarding, snowboarding, and water-skiing. The popularity of extreme sports, which originated from the West Coast, has caught on with the media and the public. It has gained coverage through the print media and the Internet, where there are web sites devoted to many aspects of extreme sports. ESPN, the major sports cable network, sponsored the first X-Games in 1995. It was a major sucess. For example, the summer games, which were held in Newport, Rhode Island, a few years back, attracted 200,000 people. After another successful X-Games in San Diego in 1998, it was announced the next X-Games will be held in San Francisco in 1999. The X-Games draw 450 of the world's best athletes in alternative sports competing in nine different sports categories.

Though not well-known compared to athletes in professional league sports, extreme sports has its share of stars, most of whom are very young. Stars in wakeboarding include sixteen-year-olds Parks Bonifay, Tara Hamilton (who won her second world title recently at the Wakeboard World Championship), Darin Shapiro, and Rob Struharik. Kelly Slater became world champion in a form of surfing called rip curl. He earned $120,600 in the Rip Curl Pro at Bell Beach in Victoria, Australia, in April 1998. His colleague Pat O'Connell is rated number two in the world of rip curl. In the area of snowboarding, Ross Power won the snowboarding half-pipe competition in the 1998 Winter X-Games, while Will Gadd won the gold medal in the ice climbing speed finals. Tina Basich and Cara-Beth Burnside placed first in their categories in Women's Snowboarding at the Winter X-Games. The fact that the games are televised on ESPN gives the sport wide exposure to audiences—the important eighteen to thirty-five-year-old male demographic—as well as attracting advertisers, such as those selling sporting goods designed for extreme sports.

Compensation varies for athletes in extreme sports. The top prize for the long-distance marathon at Badwater in Death Valley, California, was $500. Others who finished the marathon received bronze-relief belt buckles. Some athletes win big cash prizes. The Wakeboard World Championship awards $100,000 in cash and prizes. Corporate sponsorship also helps support and promote the athletes and their sport. But the excitement and surge of energy that comes from doing these death-defying feats and stunts are the overall rewards for these people who enjoy living on the edge.

**Figure Skating:** In the last few years, the world of figure skating has seen an enormous growth in popularity. In addition to huge television contracts to air various skating shows, there are also major shows, such as *Stars on Ice*, touring across the country. Many of today's top skaters tour with these shows to sold-out crowds. Skaters such as Kristy Yamaguchi and Scott Hamilton make millions on these tours, and many also have lucrative endorsement deals.

**Jai alai:** A game much like handball, but played with a curved basket fastened to the arm for catching and throwing the ball against the wall, jai alai is booming. The many frontons in Florida are open most of the year, with several games each night. Eight two-man teams usually play in one game, with players rotating partners for different games. In addition to being paid good salaries, players are also paid an extra $50 to $100 as incentive money for placing high in each game. World Jai Alai promotes an extensive training program for amateurs in Miami, Spain, and France, and a few American players are beginning to succeed. Players need the agility of a tennis player plus great skill in catching and throwing with the cesta.

**Karate:** Some tournaments pay small prizes—$100 for division winners and $1,000 for overall champions. Full-contact karate fights are staged as in boxing. The average is about $5,000 to $10,000.

Jim Coleman, editor of *Black Belt,* estimates that there are about 200 pro fighters in the United States. Beginners work up in amateur tournaments and progress from there. Women compete in tournaments but, says Coleman, "are quite rare in the full-contact arena."

**Lacrosse:** There are 750,000 lacrosse players in the United States, with 364 colleges conducting men's programs. The Major Indoor Lacrosse League, started in 1987, draws an average of 10,000 spectators per game for the six professional teams on the East Coast. Each team has twenty-three players, with rookies paid $175 per game and nine-year veterans $550 per game. The lacrosse season lasts from January to April.

**Motorcycle racing:** Professional motorcycle racing in the United States offers many purses, but none are large. The sport is more popular in Europe, where about two-thirds of the Grand Prix winners are Americans.

Many types of races are held: speedway, dirt track, road race, drag, hillclimb, indoor, and motor cross. Most racing in the United States is sanctioned by the American Motorcycle Association, so you can progress from amateur to pro in the same organization. With several thousand amateur races each year, the main problem is the expense of a motorcycle. The popular 250 class racing bike costs about $11,000. Superbikes are known to lease for as much as $400,000 per year.

Superbikes are produced by factories to boost their sales, and their riders are sponsored. Private competitors compete in club events, where the best might win as much as $90,000 in a year.

Your best opportunity for learning is on a minibike. Kenny Roberts, a legend as a rider who now works as a team boss, says, "To go faster on a GP bike, you have to brake later, flick harder, and get on the gas sooner. A minibike sharpens your timing."

Motorcycle racing is not safe. While he was still competing, Roberts said, "There is a little gear behind your brain, and any time the front wheel of the bike makes a funny slip or the back wheel slides, which is about three times a lap, this little gear tells you that you are falling down. Well, when you're eighteen that gear doesn't even work, but when you're thirty-one or thirty-two it's working so well that you aren't comfortable at the speeds you have to go to win."

**Powerboat racing:** In 1994, only fifteen professional drivers were competing in the expensive and often dangerous unlimited hydroplane races. Professional outboard racing offers more opportunity, but the half-million-dollar cost of boats provides the same difficulties as those of auto racing. Amateur competition is conducted by the American Power Boat Association, which sanctions more than 400 races each year for more than 8,000 members.

Because of the dangers involved, racers need almost reckless courage. Gold Cup champion Bill Muncey said, "Anything other than death is a minor injury."

**Racquetball:** Professional competition is not extensive, but Marty Hogan, who won close to 90 percent of his matches, earned about half a million a year in the '80s.

Racquetball requires much the same talents as tennis, with perhaps more quickness and agility and the ability to adjust to rapidly changing situations.

Like most of the individual sports, racquetball requires proficiency as an amateur before you can play in professional tournaments.

**Skiing:** Being a professional skier requires great skill and endurance. In order to become a professional, you need to be good enough to qualify to compete in the winter Olympics. Skiers improve their skills with many hours of practice, and they must be willing to devote years of their life before they can see any real money. It costs about $150 to $250 for equipment to get started. Lessons cost between $10 and $20 an hour.

The following are the top three winners of the Men's World Pro Ski Tour for the 1997–1998 season:

| | |
|---|---|
| Jokob Rhyner | $85,475 |
| Hans Hoffer | $60,725 |
| Michel Lucatelli | $40,975 |

Women compete for a substantially smaller amount of money compared to men. The following are the top three winners of the Women's World Pro Ski Tour for the 1997–1998 season:

| Isabelle Fabre | $41,068 |
| Mihaela Fera-Egan | $17,842 |
| Orphelie Racz-David | $16,365 |

**Softball:** Men's and women's pro softball began in the 1970s, but both failed. Although amateur softball now thrives, only a few professionals make a living by exhibition touring, and a women's pro league failed in 1980. The good news is that softball equipment sales amount to about half a billion dollars per year, so money is available for advertising. Craig Elliot of the Grafton, Ohio, Steeles makes about $100,000 a year in slow pitch softball. He works all week and plays several games each weekend. Many amateurs play in "bandit" tournaments where as many as twenty teams put up entry fees of as much as $250 each and play all weekend for money.

**Surfing:** The Association of Surfing Professionals has at least twenty events each year during its eleven-month season, with various prizes. Surfers collect more money for endorsements, ranging close to $200,000 for a champion. Both male and female surfers can progress through the amateur ranks.

**Tractor pulling:** Tractor pulling is popular in the Midwest and on television. Competition is for seven sizes of tractors, with multiple engines combining for more than 6,000 horsepower in tractors weighing as much as six tons. They pull sleds weighing up to 32.5

tons engineered to increase resistance as they go down the track.

In 1994, the National Tractor Pullers Association sanctioned about 350 events in the United States and Canada. Since 1978, it has been an organized sport in ten European countries. Top national pullers split about $500,000 for 1994, with more than $100,000 going to regional competitors.

**Volleyball:** Regulation six-person volleyball didn't do well as a professional sport, but it is doing well as an amateur game. In 1992, a four-person beach volleyball tour was created. However, it is facing an uncertain future. Professional two-team volleyball, especially beach volleyball, is enjoying tremendous success. Even if you are good enough to make it as a pro in volleyball, first-year players cannot expect to make much money. Many pro volleyball players have full- or part-time jobs and play in their free time. Being a professional volleyball player requires dedication and many hours of practice. It may take years before a pro volleyball player can expect to see big money.

The Association of Volleyball Professionals (AVP) conducts two-person tournaments for both men and women. Here are the leading money winners for 1997:

| *Men 1997* | | *Career Earnings* | |
|---|---|---|---|
| Jose Loiola | $318,433 | Karch Kiraly | $2,371,090 |
| Kent Steffes | $273,433 | Kent Steffes | $2,008,258 |
| Mike Whitmarsh | $161,422 | Randy Stoklos | $1,719,555 |

| *Women 1997* | | *Career Earnings* | |
|---|---|---|---|
| Lisa Arce | $55,300 | Karolyn Kirby | $458,509 |
| Holly McPeak | $55,300 | Liz Masakayan | $291,692 |
| Karolyn Kirby | $43,085 | Angela Rock | $254,459 |

The team of Lisa Arce and Holly McPeak won the bronze medal in the 1998 Goodwill Games. In 1999, the AVP will hold ten events for the women's professional tour, with more than $600,000 in prize money.

The prize money for these tours often comes from the many well-known companies that sponsor them.

**Water Skiing:** Although there are a few pro tournaments, most male and female water-ski pros earn their living from teaching or water shows. The American Water Ski Association lists about sixty-five water-ski schools, with an average of about three instructors per school.

**Wrestling:** Professional wrestling is an entertainment rather than a competitive sport, but it requires athletic development. Amateur wrestling or football are two good ways to develop strength and skill. When you think you are good enough, contact a promoter for your next step. The World Wrestling Federation attracts more than $100 million in ticket sales and $200 million in paraphernalia sales, plus many millions more from cable TV.

Of more than a thousand professional wrestlers in 1994, some earned only $50 or less for a preliminary match in a small organization, while the stars averaged about $200,000 a year. Hulk Hogan was rumored to earn close to a million dollars a year.

## AGENTS

One of the most important aspects of breaking into pro sports is getting paid. In some sports an agent can help you sign a better contract and find endorsements and appearance money for you.

You do not need an agent until you are ready to receive money for becoming a professional. In fact, if you make an agreement with an agent while you are still in college you will lose all remaining eligibility.

After you are drafted, an agent can negotiate a better contract for you. Agents also add to your income by arranging advertising contracts and personal appearances, and by giving investment and tax advice. Agents can find alternative jobs, such as in Italian professional basketball, if you cannot catch on with the top pro teams. For such services, you will pay between 3 percent and 10 percent to your agent; the average is 5 percent. Some people advise paying an agent on a job-to-job basis, since you may not need all those services at the beginning. Some athletes prefer to hire a lawyer for the contract negotiations instead of an agent. Lawyers may charge $100 an hour, so they may be cheaper and more competent at reading contracts.

You should be extremely wary of bad agents. There are thousands of agents competing for only hundreds of jobs, and often they will do whatever is necessary to get a job. They have been called "vipers" and "parasites." Jerry Vainisi, former general manager of the Chicago Bears, said, "Many are incompetent, even criminal." Ed King, a San Francisco attorney who specializes in suing agents who defraud athletes, said, "If the worst you can say about one of them is that he is incompetent, that probably puts him among the top five percent in the sports business."

Although professional sports have started to protect athletes from bad agents by certifying a list of acceptable agents, there is no such protection for rookies. Many agents try to sign college stars who are not experienced in negotiations. These agents often take advantage of the naive college athletes. Agents may offer to handle your negotiations without charge, hoping to sign you to a long contract and cash in on your future paychecks. Some agents have taken a kick-back from the negotiating team in return for signing a rookie for a smaller bonus.

Attorney Robert H. Prixin, author of *An Athlete's Guide to Agents,* advises, "Any athlete, before hiring an agent, should ask about the agent's qualifications, ethics, philosophy of representation, approach to dealing with club owners, method of calculating and collecting his fees, attitude toward renegotiation . . . ." Then after you hire an agent, Prixin advises you to "monitor the agent's performance, participate in making crucial decisions, and make sure the agent does not subordinate the player's interest to those of another client."

Others advise you to get a list of an agent's other clients and shop around before you sign. You would also be wise to select from the list of registered agents. Try to find an agent who has time for you, since some represent many athletes and are overworked. Never give an agent power of attorney. Do not sign a long-term contract. The NBA forbids its players to sign a contract with an agent for more than one year at a time. And try to find an agent who will be helpful to you after your pro career ends.

For more about agents, see the section at the end of chapter 10.

In summary, you can become a pro by finding your best sport and practicing it until you are good enough.

Each sport is structured differently, so if you want to break into a particular sport, find out what you must do to make it. Then strive to achieve those goals. Probably the best advice is: TRY HARD.

# Directing Your Pro Career

How does managing your professional career differ from managing your amateur career? If you worked extremely hard to make it into pro sports, much of your management will be the same. Many professionals realize their opportunities and learn how much harder they must work to succeed at this level, and they continue to improve. Others think they have it made and let down on their efforts, sometimes even losing their career through excesses in having fun. In addition, there are some aspects of management that do not apply to an amateur career. In any case, you can improve your life and your career success by working on each of the following areas.

## PHYSICAL CONDITIONING
Years ago baseball players used the winter months to relax. They put on weight and lost strength, speed, and endurance. A long career lasted until the age of thirty-five. Many players now spend the winter keeping in shape, and age thirty-five is regarded as a peak age rather than the end.

You have a choice as an athlete. You can try to get by with no more work than the coach forces upon you, or you can improve your conditioning throughout the year.

In addition to improving your strength, speed, and endurance, you should take care of your health. You should learn proper nutrition, avoidance of harmful habits, and prevention of injuries.

**Nutrition.** Some athletes have actually eaten themselves out of a job. The most common way is to put on extra weight, but anything that detracts from your general health will surely detract from your athletic performance.

Good nutrition is a combination of eating food that adds to your health and avoiding food that will cause your body harm sooner or later. You must consume a certain number of calories in order to survive. If many of your calories are in food that is bad for you, you suffer in two ways: you harm your body with the bad food, and you don't have room for all the good food you need.

The most important thing to learn about nutrition, then, is which foods are good for you and which ones are bad for you. Then, if you are serious about taking care of your body, you can begin to cut down on the amount of bad foods you eat and replace them with good foods.

Nutritionists generally agree on which foods are bad: fat, sugar, salt, preservatives, greasy fried foods, and any foods that bring on allergic reactions.

If you eat 44 percent of your calories in the form of fats, you are—like many Americans—in danger of developing cancer and cardiovascular problems such as heart attack and stroke. You may find it difficult to reduce your fat intake to 10 percent, but if you are serious about improving your health you will eat no more than 20 percent. You can reduce fat by avoiding red meat, butter, ice cream, and food cooked in oil. Use nonfat milk, nonfat yogurt, and nonfat cheese.

Sugar is good for you in its natural form—carbohydrates—but refined sugar is no more than concentrated calories without any nutritional value. Dr. Sheldon Reiser of Washington, DC, has done research showing that 20 percent of the adult population is at risk for heart disease from excessive sugar intake. Since sugar is so concentrated, you can obtain a large percentage of your calories from refined sugar, leaving no room for the good foods you need. Most people do not realize how much sugar is found in common foods. The worst foods are desserts, soft drinks, sugared cereals, and the sugar added to tea and coffee. One soft drink may contain six teaspoons of sugar, or 120 calories. You could literally starve to death without losing weight if you consumed nothing each day but twenty soft drinks. Excess sugar can trigger an insulin reaction, something to avoid if your ancestors had diabetes, and also can lead to the weak feeling of low blood sugar. You cannot be a good athlete if you have low blood sugar.

You need some sodium—salt—in your diet, but you can obtain more than enough in the food you eat. Excess sodium in your diet can cause high blood pressure. The quickest way to start reducing your sodium intake is to stop adding salt to your food. After a few months your taste will change and you will be happy with the natural flavor of foods.

The good foods are those that supply you with a large amount of minerals, vitamins, and fiber, plus enough protein and the essential fatty acids. In general, you can be sure you are eating well when you eat fruits, vegetables, grains, and seeds (which include beans and nuts). Your best protein choice is probably fish. Don't make the old mistake of believing that an athlete needs steak to be strong. Many of the strongest animals are vegetarians, including elephants, bulls, and rhinos. Animal proteins are usually found in food that also contains excess calories and fats. Excessive proteins overwork your kidneys and can interfere with your absorption of minerals. Dr. George L. Blackburn of Boston, Massachusetts, sets 15 percent of total calories as the upper limit for protein intake.

One possible problem arises from eliminating meat from your diet. Unless you take iron supplements you may have an iron deficiency that can reduce your endurance.

**Harm.** You can harm yourself in many ways. The most harm done by humans to their bodies comes from smoking, drinking, drugs, and other pollution such as asbestos, plus accidents. Common sense will help you avoid about 99 percent of the harm that might come to you.

**Injuries.** Sports injuries are a special kind of harm that you choose not to avoid by playing your sport. The sooner you begin to learn the causes of sports injuries, the sooner you will be able to prevent most of them.

First, you should know that injuries can result from a single violent movement or from gradual wear and tear.

You can avoid wear-and-tear injuries by paying attention. If your new shoes allow friction on your heels or toes, don't shrug off the slight burning or pink skin, because over time you will probably develop blisters or calluses. If tennis or pitching makes your elbow sore, study your movement and change enough to avoid the soreness, or something serious will develop. Aching heels can develop into bruises that will sideline you unless you wear heel cups. You should also pay attention to movements that might cause trouble. Prevention includes wearing cushioned shoes and avoiding hard surfaces when possible. Don't put up with any continued discomfort, even as slight as chafing. Your trainer cannot help you if you fail to notice that something is wrong. When you have let a minor injury progress too far and have developed a more serious problem, remember that your first step in healing is to remove the cause.

You can avoid many of the violent injuries by avoiding unnecessary risks, by using protective equipment, and by warming up properly.

Contact injuries cannot always be avoided, but you add to your chances of injury by crashing into the dugout while chasing a foul ball, diving for a passing shot in tennis, or flying into the seats to save an out-of-bounds basketball. Such hustling is spectacular and on rare occasions wins a game, but you should avoid doing it unless an important game is on the line.

Some players prefer to reduce their protective equipment to lighten their load, but you are foolish to do it against the advice of trainers, coaches, and experienced players. And not all protective equipment is good for you. A study of New Mexico high school football players found that those who wore protective braces on their knees had more than twice as many leg injuries as those who did not wear the devices. So make sure to consult a trainer before wearing or taking off a piece of equipment.

A proper warm-up includes stretching all the muscles involved in your sport and engaging in light movement to open the capillaries to your muscles. Give your body time to adjust to the stress of movement.

Your injuries will be treated by your trainer or coach or, in the case of serious injuries, by a doctor. But you can detect things no one else can. You can feel the injury, and you can judge your body's response. Only you can judge the difference between a serious, sharp injury and a soreness. The soreness will go away after a short rest and a proper warm-up, whereas a serious injury will only become worse. If a trainer is not present to treat a sudden injury, you should stop playing. Do not apply heat or cold to the injury without first consulting a trainer or physician. You could cause further harm to the injury by applying the wrong temperature pack.

You are also the best judge of when you can return to play. Never, except in the most extreme emergency, should you submit to taping and a painkiller. Pain is a warning signal; using a painkiller for an injury is like turning off the smoke alarm when your house catches on fire.

## SKILLS

You can't become a pro without excellent skills, but you must consider three facts: (1) Rarely can a skill be fully perfected by the age of twenty-three. (2) Almost all skills deteriorate if you do not practice them. (3) New skills add value to any player.

If you think a new pro cannot improve his skills, why do professional golfers, most of them over thirty years old, practice for hours each day? They even practice before and after playing a round of tournament golf. They know that the more times they swing correctly, the more certain they are of swinging correctly during competition, when one poor swing can cost thousands of dollars.

One of the problems with a skill as complex as the golf swing is the fact that you can compete, and compete well, with less than perfection. Many a professional has worked to revamp his swing after discovering some hitch that keeps him from winning. His faulty swing was good enough to get him into the pro tour, but only by perfecting it can he become a winner.

Sometimes a skill is changed without the knowledge of the player. Johnny Miller spent months doing heavy lifting around his home in the Napa Valley. As a consequence, he developed heavy muscles that changed his golf swing, and he had to work for two or three years to recover. If you work to strengthen muscles used in your skill, practice your skill at the same time to monitor and keep up with the changes.

Worse than failing to improve is letting your skills deteriorate. Can anything be worse than being careless about a skill that might earn hundreds of thousands, or even millions, of dollars? And yet many pros have done exactly that, through carelessness, laziness, or ignorance. Don't let it happen to you.

## ADD ANOTHER SKILL

Once you are a pro you may think you have enough skills, but you should think again. If you made it by doing three things well, why won't you be even better if you can do four?

When you reach the pro ranks you'll find it profitable to add new skills. Some young pitchers, even of high school age, can throw so hard that big-league batters fail to hit them. But in the major leagues, it is a rare pitcher who can survive with nothing but a fastball. Although they blasted the ball past the batter in college, they now find some of those pitches hit out of the ballpark. Many big-league pitchers became winners only after learning to throw a slider, a split-finger fast-ball, or even a knuckler.

Bob Benoit tried pro bowling for three years and had to give up. At the age of twenty-nine, he quit the tour and moved to a new city. "I needed a new game to win. If I'd stayed home, I'd have bowled with friends, gotten competitive, and never improved." He learned a hook instead of a straight ball and returned to the tour. In January 1988, he won a $27,000 first prize in the Quaker State Open and a $100,000 bonus for rolling a perfect 300.

Keep an inventory of your skills. Consider whether a new skill might add to your total ability.

## THINK

There seem to be three types of professional athletes. The most common type looks upon the profession as a good job. These athletes enjoy playing, but they also have a life to live, and they have as much fun as possible. This type may include the one who takes up the cocaine habit or the good family man with a wife and children. They all act as if they have a permanent job.

The other two types regard their job as temporary. One spends much of his or her free time working toward a future career. Pro sports offer much free time, whether between seasons or on the airplane between games.

The third type studies the sport. If you learn to think about your sport while you are an amateur, you will probably continue as a pro. Even if you are one of the first two types, you should think during competition and training in order to gain an extra edge over your competition. If you are the third type, you also think during your free time. If you become a full-time thinker, you will probably go on to become a coach or manager after you stop playing.

Part of your thinking, of course, is to monitor your progress. The principles are the same as those for your amateur career, but some of your goals will be different. For example, one of your goals should be your career after your playing days.

## PREPARE FOR YOUR FUTURE

You will want another career after your playing days end. The average professional player needs a new job by the age of thirty, but even most of the highly successful players retire by the age of forty. If you were ambitious enough and energetic enough to carve out a professional career, you will not be content with sitting around for the rest of your life.

The time to prepare for that career is while you are in college, but it is never too late. During the few years you are in pro sports, you have time to observe life around you and decide what you want to do. Then you will be wise to make some preparations. The preparations may be studying more, making contacts with people, and making plans. To motivate yourself, imagine being out of the sport with no job and nothing to occupy your time.

## AGENT

Unless you made the mistake of signing a lifetime contract with an agent, you have the opportunity to choose a new one whenever you wish. And from your contacts with other players you will have some idea of which agent you want.

Now that you are a pro, your agent is there to negotiate each new contract, to find endorsements that will
pay you well, and, if you wish, to find you speaking
engagements, sessions at training camps, interviews, or
even a book deal. If you are famous enough to command many such money-making deals, you will want a
full-time agent. If you need nothing more than a new
contract every two years, you might consider hiring an
agent for that specific purpose.

In any case, don't give your agent full authority on
your behalf. You don't want to be at home when the rest
of the team is in training camp simply because your
agent tried too hard to boost your salary. If you would
rather sign for $900,000 with the team you've been with
for your whole career than receive $1.2 million with a
team clear across the country, tell your agent your feelings before he begins. If you don't want to endorse cigarettes or liquor, tell your agent. Your agent is supposed
to work for you. You are supposed to be the boss.

## INVESTMENTS

Some of the leading moneymakers in pro sports have
died penniless. Many others have lost much of their
fortune before realizing the importance of saving and
investing. When money starts to pour in and you
believe it will continue, it is tempting to spend it.

Garry Maddox, former major leaguer, said, "There
are two kinds of *nouveau riche* athletes. Those who
spend to make up for everything they never had, and
those who want to hold on to every penny."

As soon as you receive more money than you need
for living expenses, you should make a plan. Call it a
budget if you wish, but make it definite.

First, set aside all you will need to pay your income taxes. That will amount to almost half of it. Second, set aside the amount you will need for living expenses. If your money is a bonus payment, it will not be repeated and you should budget enough for a year's living expenses.

Third, divide the remainder, saving at least half of it. You may think half is too much to save, but after taxes and living expenses, a $500,000 bonus is reduced to about $210,000, and your savings of $105,000 are only 21 percent of your bonus. On a bonus of only $100,000, your savings would be only about 10 percent.

Even if you are wise enough to save money, you can still lose it through poor investments. There are many ways to invest your savings, but your main goal is to retain all of it or possibly even make some profit from your investments. As soon as you have money, people will try to influence your investments. Many will promise returns of 20 percent a year or more, but you should remember that the higher the return, the greater your risk. Unless you are an expert and are willing to spend many hours watching your investment, you should play it safe and allow compound interest to work for you.

Compound interest is amazing. If you reinvest all the interest on your money, it will grow surprisingly. To know how many years it will take to double your money, divide 72 by your rate of interest. Thus, income of 8 percent will double your money in nine years. That means that if you saved $100,000 from your bonus at the age of twenty-three, by the time you reached fifty-nine it would have grown to $1,600,000! You are not likely to match such growth by speculating.

Young athletes are seldom prepared to invest large sums of money. You will be wise to pay a financial adviser to help you. Your agent will probably offer to be your financial adviser, but most agents are not qualified to do so. One agent went to prison for losing $1.2 million for fifty professional players in the 1970s. Another lost $6 million for fourteen athletes, and their losses may reach $15 million after IRS interest and penalties. If you earn at least an average pro salary, you will need an agent, a financial adviser, and an accountant. Be wary of combining these jobs in one person.

## MARRIAGE AND FAMILY

Most young professional athletes do not seem ready for marriage and a family. Their sudden wealth makes them think the world is their oyster, and they sow their wild oats as if they have only a year to live. Just as they fail to save money for the future and ignore the fact that they will be out of a job in a few years, they seem oblivious to what it takes to enjoy the good life in later years.

If you are wise, you will give some mature thought to the time-honored values of family life. If you do, you will sometimes conduct yourself differently. Think about it.

# Prepare for a Nonplaying Job

If you like sports, you may wish to be a glamorous, highly paid professional athlete. But if you cannot make the grade, or if you do and your career ends, you will want another career. If you would like a nonplaying career in sports, your chances are good—several hundred times better than your chances of becoming a professional athlete.

You can be connected with sports as a coach, in sports medicine, in the media, as an official, or in business. In each of those vocations your opportunities are greater if you understand sports from the player's viewpoint, especially if you made a name for yourself as a famous athlete. The demand is large for young executives who are knowledgeable about sports.

## COACH

There are more than 158,000 coaches in 19,800 U.S. high schools, thousands more in colleges, and hundreds in pro sports. About 20 percent of coaches are women.

Many high school teachers supplement their salaries by coaching. At the other end of the spectrum are coaches like Rick Pitino, who signed a contract with the Boston Celtics for $7 million per season, and Pat Riley, who was hired by the Miami Heat at a salary of $15 million over five years. Coaching can be both a fun and well-paying profession. When fringe benefits such as shoe contracts, radio-TV deals, summer camps, and speaking fees are added to salaries, it is estimated that at least a dozen college coaches receive more than $500,000, and at least fifty receive more than $250,000.

The head coach of a team is responsible for obtaining the best possible players, training them, devising game tactics, and controlling the game action as much as possible. Assistant coaches are assigned duties to help the head coach. Many high school coaches also teach classes part of the time, especially physical education classes. Coaches of individual sports, such as tennis, spend most of their time teaching individual skills and have little to do during the actual competition. To be successful, both at winning and at developing character, a coach should be a teacher and a leader, good at getting along with people and persuading them to follow instruction. With the great increase in women's sports, female coaching jobs are multiplying rapidly.

Bear Bryant, the winning coach of Alabama football, once said, "I've never recommended anybody go into coaching, 'cause if they have enough on the ball, if they can do without coaching, they should do without it. If they put as much work into it and spend as much time, the rewards are going to be much better in something else." Al Conover, former coach at Rice, said, "I'm going to become a hog farmer. After some of the things I've been through, I regard it as a step up." And Alabama basketball coach C.W. Newton said, "When a coach is hired, he's fired. The date just hasn't been filled in yet." Major League Baseball managers are fatalistic about their futures; MLB averages more than five firings per year. Sportswriter Red Smith said, "I can think of three managers who weren't fired: John McGraw of the Giants, who was sick and resigned; Miller Huggins of the Yankees, who died on the job; and Connie Mack of the Athletics, who owned the club."

Other coaches live as dangerously as baseball managers. Basketball coach Bob Zufplatz said, "Sometimes it's frightening when you see a nineteen-year-old kid running down the floor with your paycheck in his mouth." Notre Dame football coach Lou Holtz said, "A lifetime contract for a coach means if you're ahead in the third quarter and moving the ball, they can't fire you."

The conventional way to become a coach is to take education courses in college, probably specializing in physical education. You need athletic experience, and you should take public speaking to prepare you for talking to your team as well as for many public appearances. It is possible to become a coach in the pro ranks without a college education, but it is rare outside of baseball. Your chances of becoming a coach in the pro leagues are less than your chances of becoming a player, since there are five or six players for each coach and coaching careers typically last longer. If you aim for a coaching career, be sure you would like it even if you spend your life coaching in high school.

In most sports you must have some success as a high school coach before applying for a college job. And then you need even more success in college to attract attention for a pro job. In baseball, if you learn the game thoroughly and have all the coaching qualifications of leadership, you can follow a playing career with a minor-league coaching job and progress from there.

Bill Walsh's career shows how slowly even such a great coach works up in the ranks. He began as a high school coach and moved up to the university ranks three years later as a defensive coordinator. He changed universities, still an assistant, and then became an assistant coach for two pro teams. After eight years with Cincinnati, he was passed over for the head coaching job and moved to San Diego as offensive coordinator. After one year at San Diego he took the head coaching job at Stanford University for two years. His good record there won him the job as head coach of the San Francisco 49ers, twenty-two years after he started coaching.

To rise in stature as a coach, heed the words of two of the best football coaches. Vince Lombardi of the Green Bay Packers said, "Coaches who can outline plays on a blackboard are a dime a dozen. The ones who win get inside their players and motivate." Bud Wilkinson of Oklahoma said, "You can motivate players better with kind words than you can with a whip."

## GOLF PRO

One specialized category of coaching is teaching golf. Since golf is so popular and so much money is spent on playing the game, there is great demand for lessons to improve the game of the nation's amateurs, from hackers to champions.

In 1994, the 14,648 golf courses in the United States hired about 7,500 head pros, 3,000 assistant pros, and 9,000 apprentices. Assistants start at around $18,000 a year, and head pros at about $30,000. Many head pros at large clubs earn more than $100,000 a year from salary, lessons, cart fees, and shop sales. Most of them are paid something in between.

Thus, the fame and fortune go to the touring pros, but the vast majority are teaching pros. A few teaching pros play a limited amount of tournament golf.

Starting July 1, 1994, apprentices must complete three years of the new Golf Professional Training Program before being hired as pros. This course includes such subjects as rules of golf, tournament operations, teaching, interpersonal skills, club repair, golf shop management, turfgrass management, and public speaking. Costs of the GPTP are more than $2,500. In addition, the apprentice must score no higher than 15 strokes above the course rating under tournament conditions and must work for a Class A pro for six months in order to register.

To be a good teacher you need tact, enthusiasm, and patience. A golf pro also needs business skills.

## SPORTS MEDICINE

There are a few jobs for professionals who would like to specialize in sports. For example, a physician might specialize in sports medicine, or a researcher might concentrate on studies in sports physiology. Exercise physiologists might, instead of working to rehabilitate victims of auto accidents, work only with athletes.

By far, the most jobs are available to trainers. Almost all colleges and all the pro teams have an athletic trainer. There are about 10,000 trainers in the United States.

A certified athletic trainer works in six areas:

1. Prevention of injuries.
2. Recognition and evaluation of injuries.
3. Management, treatment, and disposition of athletic injuries.

4. Rehabilitation.
5. Organization and administration of the training program.
6. Education and counseling of athletes.

To become a trainer you need undergraduate work, many hours of practical work, and graduate work.

You need formal instruction in prevention, evaluation, and emergency care of injuries. You need instructional methods, health, and administration of training programs. You need courses in anatomy, physiology, kinesiology, nutrition, and psychology. Also recommended are chemistry, physics, pharmacology, statistics, and research design.

To enter the graduate program you also need 800 hours of clinical experience under a trainer certified by the National Athletic Trainers Association.

Your graduate work will include advanced study in some of the undergraduate subjects, plus sports law and 400 hours of clinical experience.

To become certified by the NATA, you must have certificates in first aid and CPR and pass the NATA Certification Examination. A teaching certificate enables you to teach and to work as a trainer with extra pay at the beginning.

The NATA has 10,000 members, but it believes that high schools offer the possibility of 10,000 to 20,000 jobs, depending upon how administrators and the public recognize the need for trainers. They estimate one million injuries among the 5.8 million high school athletes each year (636,000 in football, 126,000 in girls' basketball), and yet only 1 in 5,000 high school athletes receives comparable care. They urge athletes and their parents to ask principals, athletic directors, the medical society, and the school board to add trainers to the school athletic staff.

A trainer's most urgent duty is to give first aid during games or training. Usually a doctor is not present and the trainer substitutes, taking care of routine injuries or illnesses and sending the athlete to a physician for more serious care. A trainer does the bandaging and gives rubdowns. Some trainers become so expert in sports injuries that they can diagnose and cure these injuries better than a general physician. For example, a pitcher with a sore arm would be advised to rest by a doctor, but an experienced trainer might have him pitching in a few days. A trainer should help the athletes with preventive health care, both from injuries and from a careless lifestyle.

If you are not a star athlete and want to be a trainer, you might start as a student manager in high school or college. Your duties could be anything from water boy up to actually assisting the trainer by giving rubdowns. After your college education, you might work as a teacher and part-time trainer. With experience, the teaching duties become fewer as the trainer progresses toward a full-time job at the college or professional level.

## REPORTER

There are over 60,000 reporters and correspondents in the United States. Some work for radio, newspapers, and magazines, as well as television. Some even take on two jobs, sometimes doubling as sportswriters. Sports photographers also play an important role in sports. The average salary is $43,646, but it can be as low as $10,608 in smaller markets and as high as $106,200 in larger markets. Long hours are to be expected in this profession. Some get started early in the morning and don't finish until well into the night.

Your job as a sports reporter is to observe and report competition and to interview athletes and coaches. On small newspapers you will have extra duties whenever sports reporting is not a full-time occupation. On a newspaper, for example, a sports reporter is usually given the task of reading all the sports reports on the wire service and rewriting them according to whatever the newspaper chooses to print.

Being a sportswriter is not all fun and glamour. Red Smith said, "Writing a column is like opening a vein and letting words bleed out, drip by drip." Not all sportswriters are really experts. English sportswriter Cliff Temple wrote, "A journalist is someone who would if he could, but he can't, so he tells those who already can how they should." And sportswriters are not always favored by the athletes and coaches. Joe Paterno, the Penn State football coach, said, "If I ever need a brain transplant, I want one from a sportswriter, because I'll know it's never been used."

Some reporters work for colleges or the pros to handle publicity for their teams. Most colleges and all pro teams have a Sports Information Director. Small operations hire part-time SIDs.

As an SID you prepare handouts for any newspaper, radio station, or television people likely to report or comment on any of your games, athletes, or coaches.

To be a sports reporter or SID, you must learn to write fluently in order to turn out interesting and understandable reports in a short time. Among your high school subjects, you should take English and typing. All

**155**

jobs require someone with knowledge of sports, so a background as a competitor certainly helps, but even more important is a keen interest in sports.

If you have that interest in sports and like the idea of being a sports reporter, you can still try to progress as far as possible as a player. At the same time, some of your elective courses should be in journalism or English. You should take every opportunity to write for the school paper. One of the advantages of a writing career is that you can do it in your spare time. In high school or college you might write a sports interview and attempt to sell it to your local newspaper. Even if you fail, you will have spent your time toward improving your writing skills.

## ANNOUNCER

Television and radio sports announcers have a high earning potential. As with many jobs, when you are starting out, the pay will be on the low end of the scale. The average salary is $43,646. It can be as low as $10,608 in smaller markets, but it can be as much as $106,200 in larger markets. Big-time announcers earn salaries in the millions.

At the other end of the scale, you might start working for a radio station for as little as $100 a week. Most sports have local announcers speaking only to spectators at the scene of the event.

Radio and television employ many announcers and commentators, although they employ far fewer than newspaper reporters. On television, sports reporting for two or three minutes on the nightly news is much less than a full-time job.

To be an announcer you should have a pleasant, well-modulated voice, and for television you should also have a pleasing appearance. You should know your sport thoroughly, and it helps to be well educated and have a sense of humor.

To prepare yourself as an announcer, you might follow in the footsteps of Al Michaels. At the age of ten he decided to be an announcer, and he went around announcing everything. He turned down the audio on the television set and announced games as he watched. Following the gardener, he would give a play-by-play report: "He's put down the rake, and now he's grabbed the hose."

Announcing is not as easy as it may appear. Michaels says, "Just getting in front of the camera in front of millions of people is pressure in itself. To take an announcer's comment—one line in an entire broadcast—and then take it out of context and make him look foolish, is ridiculous. I mean, everything's ad-libbed. Johnny Carson is reading off cue cards."

Versatility is helpful when trying to break in, since many small radio stations need someone who can do several jobs. If you have a First Class Radio-Telephone Operator permit, you have an advantage because each station is required to employ one. It will also help if you can write and sell. You should take public speaking in school and do any available radio work. To break in, when you think you have something to offer, you need to apply. You might even do an interview on tape and try to interest your local radio station.

Sportscaster Paul Guanzon offers a little advice on how to break in: "It's not politics, it's just who you know."

## OFFICIAL

A few officials make a living from their work. Most of the thousands of officials, however, are part-time workers on nights or weekends, since most sports need officials for limited duty.

Officials are as vital to sports as the players. Without them, there would be no one to enforce the rules of the game. Hockey uses eight officials per game; basketball uses six, including two scorers and two timers. Baseball uses four umpires per game. The starting salary for an official is approximately $60,000. Mid-level pay is approximately $140,000, while some top officials can earn as much as $225,000. In 1997, salaries paid to officials fell between $2.2 million and $3 million. In 1999, salaries are expected to rise to $3.5 million.

An official enforces the rules of the game, often making split-second judgments. To be a good official you must know the rules, have the eyesight necessary to observe infractions, and have the impartial mind and courage to make calls against a hostile crowd. An official must be able to stand jeers and anger from the crowd. Referee Earl Strom said, "Officiating is the only occupation in the world where the highest accolade is silence."

Officials also need endurance. It is estimated that NBA referees run six miles per game. The hockey official must skate with thirty rotating players for sixty minutes.

The pro sports teams scout for officials in the same way the teams look for athletes. Therefore, you begin by officiating in amateur sports and hope to work your way up. When you decide you would like to be an official, volunteer your services as an unpaid official. Little leagues need umpires, tennis tournaments need linesmen, even some playground games use officials. In sports such as auto racing or horse racing, most officials come from people already involved in the sport. It is possible to step right into a paying job after a sports career, but it is not likely, and you'd better be extremely good.

## ADMINISTRATION

Behind the players and coaches on the playing field lies an organization necessary to the administration of sport. Somebody must handle the money necessary for preparing the playing field, for uniforms and equipment, the coach's salary, the officials' wages, travel expenses, and tickets. Somebody has to schedule the games, supervise eligibility, sell tickets, and clean the stadium. In the pro ranks, somebody has to hire coaches and sign and trade players.

Colleges large enough to have an athletic program have an athletic director who oversees most of the above duties. Some athletic directors have staff members who handle some of the responsibilities.

As far back as 1982, when all salaries were lower, the average salary for athletic directors in twenty-seven large public universities was $58,300. For fifty-three private universities, the average athletic director received $45,300. But the famous Illinois football coach Bob Zuppke says, "No athletic director holds office longer than two unsuccessful football coaches."

Pro teams have administrators who are the equivalent of athletic directors. Baseball clubs, for example, have general managers, whose most important duties include signing and trading players. The team hires other people to be business manager, ticket director, traveling secretary, and stadium director, as well as others to hold smaller administrative positions. If you want to apply, experience in a lower-level job is usually a requirement.

If you want to work toward the good salaries of athletic directors, your best method is to work first as a coach. Assistants to the athletic director may work up from lesser jobs and have a chance to become the athletic director.

In addition to college and professional teams, administrators are needed for the various leagues and conferences. Some league administrators earn large salaries. Peter Ueberroth went to work as commissioner of Major League Baseball at a salary of $450,000. Donald Fehr, executive director of the Major League Baseball Players Association, received $300,000. There is no set path for working up to such jobs. You need experience as a business executive with some connection to sports.

Another rather large field is the administration of public recreation, where a city might hire you to supervise the city's playgrounds and recreational activities. Some physical education majors also study this specialty. You will probably have to catch on as an assistant and work your way up, or enter the field from a teaching career. There is a growing demand for administrators at athletic and health clubs, and for corporate sponsorship programs.

## BUSINESS
Sports businesses can range all the way from ownership of a team down to selling programs during a game.

Sports equipment accounts for much of the sales in sports business. Thousands of sporting goods stores sell shoes, balls, clubs, rackets, clothing, books, and many other items. Some specialize in only one type of product, such as shoes or golf clubs. You should probably begin as a sales clerk and save money until you can start your own business. There is great risk of losing money in business, but a successful business will pay you more than most jobs. Your chances of success in business will improve if you study accounting and business administration.

Sports services can include almost anything, but the most popular services teach fitness and sports skills or furnish a place to play. Fitness can be taught at minimum expense by renting a hall for aerobic dancing, or you can spend a million dollars or more on a well-equipped gymnasium. Skills can be taught without great expense, but you need a thorough knowledge of the sport and of teaching methods. You can be an instructor in anything from karate to chess.

The largest capital investments in sports are for the many places to play. You might own, manage, or work for a golf course, tennis club, bowling alley, swimming pool, or any kind of sports field. The income can be large. The Pebble Beach golf course in California, for example, sends out foursomes at ten-minute intervals until about four hours before dark. They are booked months in advance at a price of $800 per foursome. Ski resorts and tennis camps also charge high fees. Where there is money, there are jobs.

More consumer money goes into golf than any other sport. Golf has gained tremendous popularity in recent years, and it owes much of this success to Tiger Woods. Woods has encouraged a new generation of young people to play the sport. Sales of golf items have increased greatly, as well as the number of people who are taking golf lessons. Because of this increased interest in the sport, golf has signed lucrative endorsement and television contracts.

Gordon Benson of the National Golf Foundation says, "The [number of golfers per year in the United States] could reach 40 million by the year 2000." Many small companies are trying to collect some of this money. If you can offer something golfers can use, you can earn some of this money for yourself.

## MISCELLANEOUS

A few opportunities do not fit into a large category, but one of them might suit your fancy.

How about being a coach of horses? They call them trainers, but they perform the same service for a race-horse as a track coach performs for runners. D. Wayne Lukas has been the top horse trainer and moneymaker for many years. In 1996, he earned almost $16 million. If you love horses and competition, it is a good job. You must start by working around the stables and by keeping your eyes and ears open while you do menial chores.

A few caddies travel the golf tour as full-time professionals. PGA Tour caddies receive a base salary of $300 to $400 a week. They also receive about 6 percent of a player's winnings, or 10 percent for a victory. This bonus amounts to as little as $100 or as much as $60,000. If you like golf that much, you can start caddying at your local golf course.

Professional teams have scouts who travel about the country watching good athletes compete in school and college games. The scout's job is to find athletes who are good enough to be signed by the pro team. You'll need a thorough knowledge of the sport, usually gained by playing for years and, sometimes, by coaching. Scouting is not a job to decide upon while you are in high school; wait until you have a professional career.

Tony Lucadello, scout for the Philadelphia Phillies, commented about the difficulties of scouting: "Unfortunately, too many parents and coaches think winning at an early age is more important than learning. I have seven guys who work for me. As a group, we see an average of 30,000 players a year. This year we saw four players who had major-league potential, only four."

Many teams, even some college teams, pay a statistician to keep records of all their players in competition. A statistician uses those raw numbers to find significant "stats" for the team. For example, when a baseball manager looks down the bench for a pinch hitter in the later innings, he keeps in mind the statistician's figures on how well each hitter has done against right- or left-handed pitchers, against this team, in this ballpark, and even in this particular inning, as well as who has been hitting the best in recent days. A statistician may not be particularly well paid, but some people are so keenly interested that they would do it for nothing, for fun.

The standard way to become a statistician is through college with training in statistics and computer programming. For details on the profession, contact the American Statistical Association, 806 15th Street NW, Washington, DC 20005. But to be an applied statistician you must know your field, so sports knowledge may be more important in your case. Certainly, your most important asset would be a consuming love of sports statistics. If you keep statistics as a hobby and find some interesting results, you can contact publications or teams that may be interested.

Nonplaying jobs in harness racing are numerous. You can be a horse breeder, a veterinarian, a trainer, a racing official, an owner, or you can be in track management.

The Professional Rodeo Cowboys Association signs contracts with announcers, rodeo secretaries, timers, pickup men, chute laborers, specialty act performers, stock contractors, and producers.

## AGENT

An agent for professional athletes can earn large sums of money. The bad news is that, since there is no limit to the number of agents, the average income is much lower than $10,000 a year for the thousands of agents. But since the registered agents represent most of the high-paid athletes, their average income is considerably higher. Unless you can beat out most of the competition or have the inside track to a great athlete, your chances of making a good living as an agent are not good. Jack Mills, one of the better independent agents, represented 414 football clients in twenty years. Some agents have only one client.

Agents wield increasing power in sports. Mark McCormack, head of the International Management Group, said, "We're by far the most powerful influence on sport in the world. We could turn any individual sport—golf, tennis, skiing—on its ear tomorrow." The IMG receives 10 percent of a player's winnings and 25 percent of endorsements.

To be an agent, you need no specific educational or professional requirements. The only regulation is registration with the NFL or NBA. Professional baseball is also beginning to require agents to register. Your best chance to break in is by handling rookies, since you do not have to be a registered agent. You need good personal salesmanship, first to sell yourself to a prospective client, and second to negotiate good contracts for your clients. You also need full knowledge of each sport, especially how much each team might be willing to pay.

The main duties of an agent are negotiating contracts and finding endorsements, but most agents take on other duties ranging from acting as financial manager down to small personal services. (One agent in Boston received a call from Honolulu asking him to get some hot water in the player's bathroom.)

Most players regard agents with favor—when they need them. Former Cincinnati pitcher Tom Seaver said, "In negotiations it's a question of whether you think they are being fair with you or trying to stick it to you. I'd rather be represented by an agent when I feel they are trying to stick it to me."

If you are not a lawyer, your best opportunities to become an athletic agent are to work for a general agency or to be so well known as a former athlete or coach that you can attract young athletes to your stable. As an athlete, you might prepare for being an agent by learning the basics of negotiating through study and practical experience.

If you love sports and are determined to work in that field, there is almost surely a place for you. Perhaps that place is not as one of the highly paid athletes, but certainly it's in a nonplaying job. Many of these jobs are not what you would call routine or standard jobs. Most are unusual, so you cannot enter them by the usual routes of school or an employment agency; you have to go to the job and present yourself as somebody who likes to do that work. Somewhere among all those strange and wonderful jobs is something for almost every sports lover.

# 11

# What's Ahead in Pro Sports?

You can never be certain about the future, neither your own nor the future of professional sports. But if you are serious about pursuing your own future as a pro you should become aware of the trends and how they may affect you.

The money that is involved in sports today is astounding. From the salaries that top professional athletes are earning, to the millions they are receiving from endorsements, to the millions that big companies are willing to pay to air commercials during sports events, it is fair to say that money and sports go hand in hand. Michael Jordan makes as much money in one season as many people will make in a lifetime. Are things getting out of control? Money was what led to the baseball strike of 1994 and to 1998's basketball lockout. When athletes and teams owners fight over money, the people who suffer the most are the fans. Only the future will tell if this trend will continue.

The following is a list of the highest paid baseball athletes for 1998:

Barry Bonds, San Francisco $11.4 million
Gary Sheffield, Florida $10 million
Albert Belle, Chicago White Sox $10 million

| | |
|---|---|
| Greg Maddux, Atlanta | $9.6 million |
| Frank Thomas, Chicago White Sox | $9.3 million |

The salaries you hear about are not always exact, for several reasons. Some secrets are better kept than others. Methods vary in computing salaries for a certain year, complicated by signing bonuses and other extra pay. In some contracts the salary changes each year.

Many players with mediocre major league records receive more than a million dollars per year. Some players who seemed to be barely hanging on to a major league job received salaries well over half a million dollars.

Salaries are also rising rapidly in basketball. The NBA is awash with money from new television contracts, and the average salary is now over $1 million.

Where does all this money come from, and will it continue?

It all started with the government's dilution of the value of the dollar. Inflation—an increase in the number of dollars in existence—has caused the dollar to buy less now than you could buy for a dime a generation ago. At the time of World War II, a millionaire was a rare individual. Now a person is apt to be called a millionaire only if his or her income reaches $1 million a year.

With billions of excess dollars in the market, the price of everything rises. Anything that is scarce has its price bid much higher because of inflation. A painting that Vincent Van Gogh could not sell during his lifetime has sold for more than $40 million. Some baseball cards have been known to sell for more than $500,000.

In addition, television contracts now pay hundreds of millions of dollars to major league teams. Players who have only recently gained the right to become free agents hire lawyers or other agents who know they have the baseball owners over a barrel. They ask for more money every year—and they often get it!

The Major League Players' Union has a useful weapon called arbitration. If a player does not get the salary increase he wants, he can "take it to arbitration." Theoretically, the arbitration is done by impartial people to arrive at a fair salary. In practice, the most common result is for the arbitrator to split the difference between the player's asking price and the owner's bid. Of course, in a few cases the player is too greedy and receives no increase, but the general result is that salaries have escalated beyond what many consider common sense. It became so bad that high-profile players have been known to demand renegotiation in the middle of contracts. They were happy with huge salaries when they signed, but when they saw other players signing for even higher salaries a year or two later, they wanted to change their agreements.

Collectively baseball players earn more than any other sport professionals. In 1991 arbitration forced baseball owners to pay players millions. As a result, a lot of the money that baseball generates goes to the players rather than the owners. The average value of baseball contracts was an astounding $8 million in 1997. The total payroll for baseball in 1997 was more than $1 billion. The average salary for a baseball player in 1997 was $1.4 million.

Baseball players' salaries vary depending on their team. The Montreal Expos pay the lowest salaries in the league, with $9.2 million, while the Baltimore Orioles pay the highest, with $70 million. Gary

Sheffield, Albert Belle, and Greg Maddux each earn more in a year than the entire Expos team.

High salaries will continue as long as the causes for them continue—inflation, the popularity of television sportcasts, the union's success in breaking the owners' lifetime hold over players, and greed. The escalation may have surged too far and may slow down, but decreases in salaries will probably come about only through major changes, such as a severe economic recession.

Other factors might reduce huge incomes to players. One important factor is fan support. Recent problems, such as strikes, franchise moves, and players complaining for more money, have alienated many fans. If not enough fans watch baseball on television, the networks might lose some of those millions that fuel the flames of price inflation. If the networks reduce the payout to the baseball clubs, salaries will take a nosedive.

Baseball's old-timers are critical of the situation. Joe Black, formerly of Brooklyn, said, "I'm waiting for the day—and I hope it never comes—that two or three teams will go bankrupt." Harmon Killebrew, who hit 573 home runs, said, "It's hard for me to believe that some of those contracts are true. It's got to stop, but I don't know when." Rusty Staub, a major league player for twenty-three years, said, "I think a lot of the owners have lost their minds."

And there are other ways the inflated salaries may be reduced. Corporations might find a more profitable way to advertise their products and thus reduce their huge payouts for endorsements. A severe recession or depression could drive people away from the high costs of sports entertainment. Until then, the trend continues to move players toward greater and greater salaries.

Another important trend in sports is the move toward control of drug use.

Laws now in effect have already made a small move in the right direction. If it lasts long enough, you will see great changes in professional sports.

Before 1983, people who wanted to eliminate drugs from sports had no more chance than those who wanted to eliminate recreational drugs from the whole populace. They knew that some athletes were cheating by using both steroids to build strength faster and stimulants to increase energy, alertness, and quickness. But they could not fight against drug use for two reasons.

Most important, too much power was lined up on the side of drug use to enhance performance. Athletes cheated to gain an advantage over their opponents. Team owners, administrators, and coaches looked the other way because they too wanted to win. This cheating went on in amateur sports such as high school athletics and in the highest ranks of professionals.

The other reason drug use was not stopped was because it was too difficult to detect the cheating. In 1983, that excuse ended when a German engineer devised a method of testing using a $30,000 gas chromatograph and a $200,000 mass spectrometer. His technology was so state-of-the-art that it effectively became accepted in all courts as being absolutely accurate in forensic medicine and toxicology.

This highly effective new tool means that no athlete can cheat by using drugs—if the tests are made.

For many years it was not illegal to use steroids. Track and field led the way both in the use of steroids and in the battle against their use. Unfortunately for track and field, the disqualification of Ben Johnson in the 1988 Olympic Games made the sport seem more tainted than others, whereas in reality the professional sports were making little or no effort to stop steroid use. In fact, steroid use by professional football players was not considered cheating until 1989. That change in the NFL law, followed by the introduction of similar regulations in other pro sports, turned the trend toward the goal of total elimination of drugs from sports.

The incentive to cheat still remains, but the trend is toward catching cheaters. The only roadblock that remains is dishonesty among those who run the various sports, so it seems inevitable that the situation will improve. To stop the cheating, now that we have the laws and the technology, we need the will of the leaders and athletes.

That will to control drugs in sports may be strengthened as more states pass laws that classify steroids under Category II of the Controlled Substances Act of 1970. Users will thus be criminals, and owners and coaches who condone use will be accessories.

A *New York Times* article in August 1993 stated that the NFL makes a preseason test and 6,000 random tests each year, but not one roster player has ever tested positive since November 1991. This has happened despite the fact that some players told the NFL that a "significant number of players" use steroids and that those players can easily fool the testers. They would not be able to fool blood tests on the day of the game, but apparently the NFL is not serious enough about the issue to implement such tests. In fact, the NFL commissioner says the League does not have a steroid problem.

The 1998 Tour de France faced many problems concerning drugs. The top-ranked Festina team was thrown out of the tour after the team masseur was found with a carload of banned substances. Team members and officials admitted to using banned substances. Another six teams were under suspicion for drug use.

Professional soccer showed itself to be a leader in ending drug use among players in 1991 by barring its most famous player. Diego Maradona was suspended for fifteen months because he used cocaine before a game.

Most athletes would not risk their health if they knew their opponents were also clean. Most coaches and owners would feel the same. Fans would be just as happy knowing that athletes were drug-free. The only losers would be the sellers of the drugs and steroids, who would lose millions, and the cheaters, who would lose their careers. It is hoped that the trend toward drug-free sports will continue.

It is quite possible that athletes starting their high school sports careers in 1997 without drugs will develop into the best professionals of 2010 simply because they learned to compete without artificial help. Those who use the crutch may fall when the crutch is removed.

Another trend has to do with agents. The large number of agents trying to make a killing off the abilities of athletes includes some agents who are capable and ethical. Some, however, are not. One agent, Mel Levine, claims that the agents are not the only guilty party. Levine, who recruited more than fifty undergraduates between 1981 and 1988 (against NCAA regulations) and "advanced" them money, says, "Students should know the rules and understand the consequences. Let the student culprits also pay the price." He advocates the forfeiting of scholarships, expulsion from school, and repayment of the used portion of the scholarship for students who wrongfully and knowingly violate regulations.

International Management Group, the largest agency, has also been subjected to criticism. The IMG bought the tennis academy that produced Pete Sampras, Andre Agassi, and Jennifer Capriati and uses it to turn out as many future clients as possible. The size of their business might be judged by a prediction about one of their twelve-year-old students, made on *60 Minutes* in October 1994. The girl is expected to earn $5 to $15 million a year before she is eighteen, netting millions each year for IMG. Tennis commentator Bud Collins said, "IMG has a tremendous stranglehold on the game," calling it "unconscionable . . . like drug pushers on the playground." Collins declared, "I don't think any agent should be able to talk to a youngster until that youngster has graduated from high school."

New rules need to be made and probably will be. And present rules need more enforcement. Young future pros need to be protected from unethical agents and need to practice honesty before it is forced on them the hard way.

A trend has started toward personal security for players. After Monica Seles was stabbed during a tennis match, players in other sports have become more concerned. The assault on figure skater Nancy Kerrigan also opened the eyes of other famous athletes. Some have hired bodyguards. Teams and leagues are becoming aware of the spreading danger. The NFL has made a rule against guns "on the premises." Along with increasing lawlessness throughout the United States, players in the spotlight will be at risk.

Another trend may be the continuation of periodic strikes by the players' unions. Strikes are certain to gain higher pay for the players, union officials, and lawyers, but there are two sides to the battle. Players are not paid while they are on strike, so the highest-paid players will think twice about giving up a job that pays up to $50,000 an hour. As pro football players learned, hundreds of good "scabs" are ready, willing, and able to play. The fans would rather watch the established stars, but they have already paid for their season tickets and the season will go on. The owners will fight back, so there will be opportunities for players who are not quite good enough for the big leagues. Strikes will increase opportunities for players who are not yet ready for the major leagues, the NFL, the NBA, or the NHL.

Marvin Miller, who built the powerful Major League Players' Union, explained the reasoning behind the 1994 baseball strike at the time of the strike: "Baseball's total revenue continues to grow by leaps and bounds every year. Baseball through 1993 [set] all-time records for attendance ten times in twelve years." But others say at least twelve teams lost money in 1993.

In other words, the reasoning is the same as that of bank-robber Willie Sutton. When asked, "Why do you rob banks?" Sutton replied: "That's where the money is."

In football, on the other hand, the NFL set a salary cap for each team, and many teams had to let go of high-salaried players in 1994 in order to stay under the ceiling.

Perhaps there will be a better way in the future. Perhaps the owners and the players can agree on a certain percentage of the revenue to go to players. Then their total salaries would not be known until the end of the year. In some years there would be pleasant bonuses. In a bad year they would receive less money. The players could not kill the goose that lays the golden egg, and the owners could not squeeze the players unfairly.

One trend that has been moving strongly for a few years will probably continue: players will try harder. Many fans think players let down after signing those huge contracts, but think about it; most of them want another big contract after two or three years when this one expires. Most of them play for pride as well as money. And if they let down too much they can be released. For the players who think they have a chance at one of those incredible salaries, there is no way but to try harder. And the younger players know that the only way to get ahead of a rival with equal ability is to try harder.

Thus, the trend is for players to train harder and to play smarter by spending more time thinking. Not many years ago baseball players took time off for half a year between seasons, relying on spring training to put them in shape to play. Now more and more of them have replaced hunting and fishing with running and weight training. The dazzling salary increases make this trend a certainty.

The huge increase in money has started a trend toward more teams in each sport. The desire is there, from eager communities all over the nation, and the money is there. The National League added two teams in 1993. For their June 1996 draft, the NBA had twenty-seven teams. When Disney wanted to add a hockey team to the NHL in 1993, they paid the league a franchise fee of $50 million. Half of that went to the Los Angeles Kings for allowing the Mighty Ducks to enter their territory. The result of this trend is more opportunities for more pro athletes.

Apparently more and more money will be showered upon athletes. Tonya Harding, the disgraced ice skater who admitted to covering up her friends' attack on Nancy Kerrigan before the 1994 Winter Olympics, was paid $600,000 from *Inside Edition* for exclusive rights to interview her on television.

Rick Plata, advertising executive, said, "You may think America doesn't need any more sports, but we've found the appetite is insatiable."

The trend is definitely toward more professional players. Where they will play is anybody's guess. If baseball and football catch on in foreign countries, the possibilities are staggering. If some of the money is put into women's sports, we may see a doubling of the number of professionals. You can be almost certain that more people will become professional athletes.

However, much of this expansion of players has come and will continue to come from athletes outside the United States. Foreign tennis players have been dominating the sport for years.

Prize money for golf in foreign countries now rivals that in the United States. Many former Eastern Bloc hockey players are now in the NHL, and several basketball stars from Europe are in the NBA. This particular trend may cut down on the opportunities for U.S. athletes.

In addition to the expansion of present sports, the large supply of money and spectator interest is almost sure to bring out new ideas from entrepreneurs intent upon cashing in. There may be more special TV events, staging competition solely for the television audience. Hundred-meter dashes pitting football players against track men appear too one-sided in favor of track's sprinters, but what would happen if they had to run around posts as in a slalom race? And how would Michael Jordan and other high leapers in the NBA do against trained high jumpers? Such ideas are for established stars, but somebody might even invent a whole new sport. That would increase the number of opportunities for athletes, coaches, team owners, and anyone with a good idea.

Coaches are starting to receive salaries more in line with those of their players. Nets coach John Calipari is a perfect example with his contract for $15 million.

One entrepreneur, Stephen Austin, started something new in 1989 with his Scout Camp. In the spring of 1991, about 1,300 hopeful football players paid $95 each plus expenses to be evaluated as prospective professional football players. They were tested for speed, strength, and skills, and reports were sent to the pro teams. Scout Camp shows the possibility of new ideas, and it gives an opportunity to more football players, even though only 10 percent of them will receive tryouts at a pro training camp.

No one is ever certain about the future, but the trend is definitely toward bigger and better professional sports, with more and more money available. Most of the money will go to players and management, but the fringe jobs will also thrive. Your chances are better than ever.

# Summing Up

Now that you have considered most of the factors involved in becoming a successful pro, it is time to stop for a moment and consider the whole picture. You need to think about your whole life and how your sports career fits into it.

Think about what you want out of life. Most people want to make a secure living, preferably working at a job they enjoy. The majority want love, marriage, and a family. Everybody wants some fun out of life, including friends and a wide choice of entertainment. Everybody has dreams of fame and fortune. It is up to you to set your own goals, but for many people those goals include a career, marriage, and fun.

When you first begin playing a sport, you do it for fun. As a beginner, you have fun learning and playing. If you have natural ability and play well, you will make the team in high school, and if you improve and become better than average, you will do the same in college. Most would do this even if there were no such thing as professional sports.

Many students believe that college is a time for fun and parties. They go all the way through college without making the effort necessary to succeed. They party their way through college with little thought to the future. After four years, when everyone else has earned their degrees or found jobs, these party-goers have nothing to show for their years at college. It's the same if you go through college concentrating on sports and nothing else. College should not be a vehicle for you to become a professional athlete. If you are injured in a game or you don't make it into your sport, what will you do with the rest of your life? How will you make a living? You have only yourself to blame for not earning the education you need to succeed in your future life.

As fewer young athletes stay in college to earn their degrees, it becomes more difficult for others to focus on getting an education both on and off the court. Especially in sports like basketball, hockey, baseball, and football, in which exceptional young players are highly sought out by pro teams and fans alike, athletes are leaving college early, or even skipping college altogether, to enter the pro ranks. Now young athletes have to make a difficult decision, usually under the intense scrutiny of the media, between earning their college degree and making big money in the pros. It is a very risky decision. On one hand, it could turn out very well, as was the case with Michael Jordan, who left the University of North Carolina after his sophomore year for a long and successful career in the NBA. On the other hand, it could end in disaster if you fail to succeed in the pros and have no other skills to fall back on. So before you take that step and sacrifice your college years, be sure that you have what it takes for a long career in professional sports.

It is all right to have a dream. You can dream of being a famous athlete and making a fortune doing it, but be sure you also develop other aspects of your life. If you put all your eggs in one basket by concentrating only on sports, you will have little to fall back on should you not make it as a pro.

You have read about the highs and lows of a career in pro sports. The glory and the fame that professional sports can offer will take a great amount of dedication and perseverance to achieve. If you are willing to put in this effort and if you have strong natural abilities, you are sure to become a success. Go for it!

# Glossary

**accuracy** The ability to perform an action with absolute correctness, as to hit the bull's-eye of a target.

**agility** The ability to move easily and quickly through a series of motions that make up a skill, such as juggling or dancing.

**anaerobic** Occurring only in the absence of oxygen; exercises that do not deplete the supply of oxygen.

**capillaries** The smallest blood vessels, which form a network throughout the body.

**circuit training** Program of exercises designed so that one part of the body rests while another is in movement.

**concentration** Direction of one's attention to a single object or goal with a view to achieving excellence.

**coordination** The ability to control the movement of muscles in order to accomplish a physical task.

**endurance** The ability to continue a stressful physical activity over a period of time.

**glycogen** The form in which carbohydrates are stored in the muscles and liver and used as fuel.

**isometric** Involving contraction of muscles when exerted against an immovable object, increasing muscle tone.

**kinesthesia** A sense that informs the brain of the position of body parts.

**potential** The innate ability of a person to succeed as opposed to conscious efforts to reach certain goals.

**quickness** Rapidity of reaction and movement; immediate response, as opposed to speed of motion as in running.

**reflex** Reaction to a stimulus without conscious thought, activated by a nerve impulse.

**resistance training** Exercising muscles against opposition by a force, as in sprinting up a hill instead of on a level ground.

**steroids** Synthetic hormones used illegally in attempts to bulk up body muscles and increase strength.

**stimulus** Something that causes a reaction in the body or a part of it, such as shivering in a cold wind.

**weight training** Increasing muscle mass and strength by working out with barbells.

# For More Information

You can obtain specific information about your sport from books, from magazines, and from the associations governing the sport and assisting its athletes. Most books and magazines are of limited help, but they are interesting to anyone in that particular sport. Ask your librarian for lists. Below are samples of associations and publications:

**Arm Wrestling**
International Federation of Arm Wrestling
4219 Burbank Boulevard
Burbank, CA 91505
(818) 953-2222
Fax: (818) 953-2220

**Auto Racing**
Championship Auto Racing Teams (CART)
755 West Bid Beaver Road, Suite 800
Troy, MI 48084
(810) 362-8800

National Hot Rod Association
2035 Financial Way
Glendora, CA 91741
(818) 914-4761

National Association for Stock Car Auto Racing
801 International Speedway Boulevard
P.O. Box 2875
Daytona Beach, FL 32120
(904) 253-0611

Sports Car Club of America
P.O. Box 3278
Englewood, CO 80112
(303) 694-7222
Fax: (303) 694-7391

*Driving schools:*
Stephens Racing School of High Performance Driving
2232 South Nogales Street
Tulsa, OK 74107
(918) 583-1136
Fax: (918) 583-1135

**Baseball**
Major League Baseball Players Association
12 East 49th Street
New York, NY 10017
(212) 826-0808

**Basketball**
National Basketball Players Association
1700 Broadway, Suite 1400
New York, NY 10019
(212) 333-7510
Fax: (212) 956-5687

**Billiards**
Billiard Congress of America
1700 First Avenue South, Suite 25A
Iowa City, IA 52240
(319) 351-2112
Fax: (319) 351-7767
Web site: http://www.netins.net/showcase/beahome

Professional Billiards Tour Association
4412 Commercial Way
Spring Hill, FL 34606
(352) 596-7868

**Boating**
American Power Boat Association
P.O. Box 377
Eastpointe, MI 48021
(810) 773-9700
Fax: (810) 773-6490
Web site: http://www.goracing.com

Super Boat Racing
1323 20th Terrace
Key West, FL 33040
(305) 296-8963
Fax: (305) 296-9770

**Bowling**
Ladies Pro Bowlers Tour
7171 Cherryvale Boulevard
Rockford, IL 61112
(815) 332-5756
Fax: (815) 332-9636

Professional Bowlers Association
P.O. Box 5118
1720 Merriman Road
Akron, OH 44334-0118
(330) 836-5568
Fax: (330) 836-2107
Web site: http://www.pba.org

**Boxing**
Golden Gloves Association of America
8801 Princess Jeanne NE
Albuquerque, NM 87112
(505) 298-8042
Fax: (505) 298-1191

**Chess**
U.S. Chess Federation
186 Route 9W
New Windsor, NY 12553

**Coach**
Scholastic Coach
555 Broadway
New York, NY 10012-3999
(212) 343-6370
Fax: (212) 260-8587

**Cycling**
National Cycle League
532 La Guardia Place
New York, NY 10012
(212) 260-7424
Fax: (212) 777-3611

**Fishing**
Bassing America Corp.
P.O. Box 796908
Dallas, TX 75379-6908
(214) 380-2656
Fax: (214) 380-2621

**Football**
Canadian Football League
110 Eglinton Avenue W
Toronto, ON M4R 1A3
(416) 322-9650
Fax: (416) 322-9651

NFL Players Association
2021 L Street NW
Suite 600
Washington, DC 20036
(202) 463-2200

National Football League
280 Park Avenue
New York, NY 10017
(212) 450-2000

**Golf**
PGA Tour
112 TPC Boulevard
Ponte Vedra, FL 32082
(904) 285-3700
Fax: (904) 285-7913

Ladies PGA
100 International Golf Drive
Daytona Beach, FL 32114
(904) 274-6200
Fax: (904) 274-1099

**Golf Pro**
Professional Golfers' Association of America
P.O. Box 109601
100 Avenue of the Champions
Palm Beach Gardens, FL 33418
(407) 624-8400
Fax: (407) 624-8452

**Harness Racing**
U.S. Trotting Association
750 Michigan Avenue
Columbus, OH 43215
(614) 224-2291
Fax: (614) 224-4575

**Hockey**
American Hockey League
425 Union Street
West Springfield, MA 01089
(413) 781-2030
Fax: (413) 733-4647
Web site: http://www.canoe.ca/ahl

East Coast Hockey League
125 Village Boulevard
Plainsboro, NJ 08536
(609) 452-0770

International Hockey League
1577 North Woodward Avenue, Suite 212
Bloomsfield, MI 48304
(810) 258-0580
web site: http://www.theihl.com

NHL Players Association
777 Bay Street, Suite 2400
Toronto, ON M5G

**Horse Racing**
The Jockey's Guild Inc.
250 West Main Street, Suite 1820
Lexington, KY 40544-4230
(606) 259-3211
Fax: (606) 252-0938

United States Trotting Association
750 Michigan Avenue
Columbus, OH 43215
(614) 224-2291

**Karate**
Black Belt
P.O. Box 918
Santa Clarita, CA 91380-9018
(805) 257-4066
Fax: (805) 257-3028
Web site: http://www.blackbeltmag.com

**Lacrosse**
Major Indoor Lacrosse League
2310 West 75th Street

Prairie Village, KS 66208
(913) 384-8960
Fax: (913) 384-8961

U.S. Lacrosse
113 West University Parkway
Baltimore, MD 21210
(410) 235-6882

**Motorcycling**
American Motorcyclist Association
P.O. Box 6114
Westerville, OH 43081-6114
(800) AMA-JOIN
Fax: (614) 891-5012

**Rodeo**
International Pro Rodeo Association
P.O. Box 83377
Oklahoma City, OK 73148
(405) 235-6540
Fax: (405) 235-6577

Professional Rodeo Cowboy Association
101 Pro Rodeo Drive
Colorado Springs, CO 80919

**Sports Information Director**
College Sports Information Directors of America
Campus Box 114A
Kingsville, TX 78363
(512) 595-3908
Fax: (512) 592-0389

## Skiing
Pro Skiing U.S.A.
P.O. Box 680
Bath, ME 04530
(207) 443-2743

## Sled Dog Racing
International Sled Dog Racing Association
P.O. Box 446
Nordman, ID 83848
(208) 443-3153
Fax: (208) 443-3052

## Soccer
Continental Indoor Soccer League
16027 Ventura Boulevard
Encino, CA 91436
(818) 906-7627
Fax: (818) 906-7693
E-mail: cislpr@aol.com

Major League Soccer
110 East 42nd Street, Suite 1502
New York, NY 10017
(212) 450-1200

National Professional Soccer League
115 Dewalt Avenue, NW
Canton, OH 44702
 (330) 455-4625
Fax: (330) 455-3885
E-mail: npsll@aol.com

## Softball
Women's Professional Fastpitch
46 East Fourth Street
Minneapolis, MN 55101
(612) 335-8835

## Tennis
ATP Tour
200 ATP Tour Boulevard
Ponte Vedra Beach, FL 32082
(904) 255-5000
Fax: (904) 285-5966
Web site: http://www.atptour.com

World Team Tennis
445 North Wells, Suite 404
Chicago, IL 60610
(312) 245-5300
Fax: (312) 245-5321

## Tractor Pulling
World Pulling International, Inc.
6969 Worthington-Galena Road
Worthington, OH 43085
(614) 436-1761
Web site: http://www.goracing.com

## Track and Field
USA Track & Field
P.O. Box 120
Indianapolis, IN 46206-0120
(317) 261-0500
Fax: (317) 261-0481

Track & Field News
2570 El Camino Real, Suite 606
Mountain View, CA 94040
(415) 948-8188
Fax: (415) 948-9445
E-mail: tfnmail@aol.com
Web site: http://www.olympic.nbc.com

**Trainer**
National Athletic Trainers' Association
2952 Stemmons Freeway
Dallas, TX 75247
(214) 637-6282
Fax: (214) 637-2206
Web site: http://www.nata.org

**Volleyball**
Association of Volleyball Professionals
330 Washington Boulevard, Suite 600
Marina del Rey, CA 90292
(310) 577-0775
Fax: (310) 577-0777

Great Western Team Cup Volleyball
3900 West Manchester Boulevard
Inglewood, CA 90305
(310) 419-3257
Fax: (310) 677-5671

National Volleyball Association
1001 Mission Street
South Pasadena, CA 91030
(800) 682-6820
Fax: (800) 5-SPIKER

Women's Professional Volleyball Association
840 Apollo Street, Suite 205
El Segundo, CA 90245
(310) 726-0700
Fax: (310) 726-0719
Web site: http://www.volleyball.org/wpva

**Wrestling**
World Wrestling Federation
P.O. Box 3857
Stamford, CT 06902
(203) 352-8600
Fax: (203) 359-5109

# For Further Reading

**Announcer**

McKay, Jim, and Jim McPheee. *The Real McKay.* New York: E. P. Dutton, 1998.

Miller, Jon. *Confessions of a Baseball Purist.* New York: Simon and Schuster, 1998.

Smith, Curt. *Of Mikes and Men: Broadcast Tales from the Pro Football Booth.* South Bend, IN: Diamond Communications, 1998.

**Coach**

Chambers, Dave. *Coaching: Winning Strategies for Every Level of Play.* Buffalo, NY: Firefly, 1998.

Phillip, Joan, and Jerry Wilkerson. *Teaching Team Sports: A Coed Approach.* Champaign, IL: Human Kinetics Inc., 1998.

Rooney, John F. *The Recruiting Game.* Lincoln, NE: University of Nebraska Press, 1980.

Sabcock, Ralph J., PhD. *The Coach.* Philadelphia: W.B. Saunders, 1973.

Smith, E. Simpson. *Bear Bryant.* New York: Walker and Co., 1984

Warren, William E. *Coaching and Control: Controlling Your Program, Your Team, and Your Opponent.* New York: Prentice Hall, 1997.

## Official

O'Bryant, Michael C. *Making It As a Sports Official.* Reston, VA: American Alliance For Health Physical Education, Recreation, and Dance, 1991.

*Sports Officiating Career Handbook: You Call The Shots.* Cleveland: L. R. Pub, 1997.

## Training

Nelson, Cordner. *Excelling in Sports: How to Train.* New York: Rosen Publishing Group, Inc., 1985.

Avila, Patricia G. *Olympic Sports and Fitness: A Gold Medal Guide to Improved Strength, Aerobic Fitness, Flexibility, Weight Control and Performance.* Woodacre, CA: Penmarin Books, 1998.

Griswold, John. *Basic Training: A Fundamental Guide to Fitness for Men.* New York: St. Martin's Press, 1998.

Siedentop, Daryl. *Introduction to Physical Education, Fitness, and Sport.* Mountainview, CA: Mayfield Publishing Company, 1997.

## Careers in Sports

Carter, David M. *You Can't Play the Game If You Don't Know the Rules: Career Opportunities in Sports Management.* Manassas Park, VA: Impact Publications, 1994.

Fischer, David. *The 50 Coolest Jobs in Sports: Who's Got Them, What They Do, and How You Can Get One!* New York: ARCO Publications, 1997.

Fried, Gil, and Lori Miller. *Employment Guide for Sport, Recreation, and Fitness.* Durham, NC: Carolina Academic Press, 1998.

Reeves, Diane L. *Career Ideas for Kids Who Like Sports.* New York: Facts on File, 1998.

## Statistics/Facts

Bennett, Jay. *Statistics in Sports.* New York: Oxford University Press, 1998.

Cohen, Neil. *Everything You Want to Know About Sports Encyclopedia.* New York: Bantam Doubleday, 1994.

## Other Topics Related to Sports

Hassan, John, and Chris Berman. *1998 ESPN Information Please? Sports Almanac.* New York: Hyperion, 1997.

Youngblut, Shelley. *Did You Know?: Ultimate Sports Trivia Book.* New York: Hyperion, 1998.

——— . *Way Inside ESPN's X Games.* New York: Hyperion, 1998.

# Index